# wisconsin
# Farm Lore
## Kicking Cows, Giant Pumpkins
## & Other Tales from the Back Forty

MARTIN HINTZ

THE
History
PRESS

www.historypress.net

Copyright © 2012 by Martin Hintz
All rights reserved

First published 2012

ISBN 978.1.5402.2112.4

Library of Congress CIP data applied for.

*To all the ancestors who were farmers. And to the next generation.*

# Contents

Acknowledgements       7

The Land       9
The People       39
The Animals       81
The Crops       98
The Products       123

Notes       143
Bibliography       149
About the Author       159

# Acknowledgements

The author wishes to thank the many folks who provided assistance on this book, including farmers, stock breeders, librarians, authors, educators, marketers, agricultural association representatives, federal/state/county professionals, scientists and farm organizations. Their help was invaluable. Special thanks also to my wife and farming partner, Pam Percy.

# The Land

*No other human occupation opens so wide a field for the profitable and agreeable combination of labor with cultivated thought, as agriculture.*
*—Abraham Lincoln*[1]

## WISCONSIN'S TOPOGRAPHY

Wisconsin is noted for its natural beauty and rich resources. Shaping of the landscape is attributed to the hard, grinding work of glaciers thousands of years ago:

> *For preparing Wisconsin to be the abode of a great civilization… glacial action was significant in several ways. It tended to "iron out" the rougher, hilly surfaces; it made the flat lands more rolling by creating elevations of glacier-bone materials upon them; it made soil and distributed it over vast areas…for the purposes of agriculture, it was almost as fortunate that the flat lands were made more uneven as that the rough lands were made more smooth. A gently rolling surface affords natural drainage, for the want of which much flat land becomes waste in unfavorable seasons. Besides, the glacial hills and hillocks—the moraines, drumlines,*

*kames, and eskers (to borrow the geologist's terms)—diversify the surface, vary the tree growth, and account for much of the natural beauty for which Wisconsin is so justly famed.*[2]

# JUNEAU OPENS TRACTS FOR SETTLEMENT

Noted Wisconsin entrepreneur Solomon Juneau bought up several tracts of land around what was then Washington City. He parceled them out to eager settlers who were starting to flood into Wisconsin from the East and overseas. Their plows slowly tamed the earth, forcing Chief Waubeka and the last of the Potawatomi nation from the area in 1845. One land section of Juneau's holdings eventually became part of the original Afterglow Farm acreage, owned by the Uihlein family. A copy of a Juneau deed remains in the their archives.

*Certificate No. 469*

*The United States of America*
*To all to whom these presents shall come, Greeting:*

*Whereas, a Certificate of the Register of the Land Office at Milwaukee, Wisconsin, has been deposited in the General Land Office, whereby it appears that full payment has been made by the claimant Solomon Juneau according to provisions of the Act of Congress of April 24, 1820, entitled "An Act making further provision for the sale of public lands," and the acts supplemental thereto, for the northeast fractional quarter of Section Two in Township eleven north of Range twenty-two east of the Fourth Principal Meridian, Wisconsin, containing one hundred forty-four acres and twenty-eight hundredths of an acre, according to the Official Plat of the Survey of the said Land, returned to the General Land Office by the Surveyor General.*

*Now Know Ye, that United States of America, in consideration of the premises, and in conformity with the several Acts of*

*Congress in such case made and provided, has given and granted and by these presents does give and grant, unto the said claimant and to the heirs of the said claimant the Tract above described: to have and to hold the same, together and with all the rights, privileges, immunities, and appurtenances, of whatsoever nature, thereunto belong, unto the said claimant and to the heirs and assigns of this said claimant forever.*

*This patent is issued in lieu of one dated June 20, 1837, which has been canceled, because the land was erroneously described as in Section five, instead of said Section two.*

*In testimony whereof, I, Franklin D. Roosevelt, President of the United States of America, and cause these letters to be made Patent, and the Seal of the General Land Office to be hereunto affixed, given under my hand, at the City of Washington, the thirteenth day of August, in the year of our Lord one thousand nine hundred and thirty-five, and the Independence of the United States the one hundred and sixteenth.*

*By the President: Franklin D. Roosevelt (signature)*
*By Louise Polk Wilson, Secretary (signature)*
*Ruth Sackett, Recorder of the General Land Office (signature)*
*Recorded: Patent Number 1077656[3]*

## BUYING A FARM

The following advertisement comes from H.R. McCullough and W.B. Kniskern, general pass and ticket agents. It is typical of early promotions used to lure would-be farmers dreaming of owning their own acreage.

*Why pay rent. Better own a farm. Start Now! Thousands of acres of fertile lands, capable of raising the finest quality of farm products in luxurious abundance are for sale, upon reasonable terms in Wisconsin, Minnesota, South Dakota, Iowa, Nebraska and Wyoming. Referent to reliable statistics will demonstrate the fact that the pursuits of agriculture, stock raising, and dairying in these States are attended with profitable results. Chicago & Northwestern Railway affords easy access to unfailing markets. Correspondence solicited from intending settlers. Send for free copy of "The North-Western Home seekers."*[4]

# CLEARING AN EARLY FARM

Pioneers were confronted with many challenges when arriving at their homesteads. It wasn't just a process of tossing seeds into the ground. Even before the land could be planted, it needed to be cleared of timber and brush and then tilled. In the days before major farm implements, this was backbreaking work, requiring long hours and strong muscles:

*Early Wisconsin settlers preferred a combination of prairies and oak openings. With four or five yoke of oxen, they could break two or three acres of prairie sod a day and they could get needed timber from the oak groves. Yet many of the settlers took heavily forested land in cases where it was the only thing conveniently available to them or where it had advantages of location (nearness to a market, a lake port, or a railroad). A pioneer with such land might pardonably have been discouraged as he confronted the thick growth of pine, maple, beech, and basswood, many of the trees five or six feet in diameter and some of them over a hundred feet tall. In a whole year, he and his family could clear no more than six or seven acres, and he would still have the task of breaking the land to the plow.*

*On a new farm, the pioneer as a rule planted corn for his first crop, to feed himself, his family, and his oxen. But he intended to be a commercial farmer as son as he could. He needed a cash crop, and his best bet was wheat (spring wheat). This he could not only be sure of selling but would also find comparatively easy to grow. After plowing and sowing, scattering the seed by hand, he could leave the field unattended till harvest time. True, harvesting was something of a problem, for with a scythe and cradle he could cut only two or three acres of the ripe grain a day. But he could take care of a much larger crop if he could afford to buy or rent one of the horse-drawn mechanical reapers that the McCormick company had begun to manufacture.*[5]

## LAND FOR POOR FARM PURCHASED

A poorhouse was a government-run facility for the housing of dependent or needy persons, often the elderly. These were typically run by a county or municipality in the days before Social Security. Typically, those who were still able to labor in the fields were required to do so. "Going to the poor farm" was usually considered a term of opprobrium, especially for proud, hardworking men and women who had fallen on hard times.

On September 27, 1851, land was purchased for a poor farm to be located in the town of Yorkville, near Racine.[6]

## ABE SPEAKS UP FOR AGRICULTURE

When Abraham Lincoln gave this speech before the Wisconsin State Agricultural Society on September 30, 1859, he was already seen as the rising Republican politician who debated Stephen Douglas. He was elected president a year later and, two years afterward, signed the bill establishing the United States Department of Agriculture.

Lincoln exhorted his audience to "prefer" what he called free labor, with "its natural companion, education." He saw agriculture as an opportunity for "cultivated thought," saying, "Every blade of grass is a study; and to produce two, where there was but one, is both a profit and a pleasure."

*Agricultural Fairs are becoming an institution of the country; they are useful in more ways than one; they bring us together, and thereby make us better acquainted, and better friends than we otherwise would be. From the first appearance of man upon the earth, down to very recent times, the words "stranger" and "enemy" were quite or almost, synonymous. Long after civilized nations had defined robbery and murder as high crimes, and had affixed severe punishments to them, when practiced among and upon their own people respectively, it was deemed no offence, but even meritorious, to rob, and murder, and enslave strangers, whether as nations or as individuals. Even yet, this has not totally disappeared. The man of the highest moral cultivation, in spite of all which abstract principle can do, likes him whom he does know, much better than him whom he does not know.*

*To correct the evils, great and small, which spring from want of sympathy, and from positive enmity, among strangers, as nations, or as individuals, is one of the highest functions of civilization. To this end our Agricultural Fairs contribute in no small degree. They make more pleasant, and more strong, and more durable, the bond of social and political union among us. Again, if as Pope declares, "happiness is our being's end and aim," our Fairs contribute much to that end and aim, as occasions of recreation—as holidays. Constituted as man is, he has positive need of occasional recreation; and whatever can give him this, associated with virtue and advantage, and free from vice and disadvantage, is a positive good. Such recreation our Fairs afford. They are a present pleasure, to be followed by no pain, as a consequence; they are a present pleasure, making the future more pleasant.*

*But the chief use of agricultural fairs is to aid in improving the great calling of agriculture, in all its departments, and minute divisions—to make mutual exchange of agricultural discovery, information, and knowledge; so that, at the end, all may know every thing, which may have been known to but one, or to but a few, at the beginning—to bring together especially all which is supposed to not be generally known, because of recent discovery, or invention.*[7]

# UW Regents Support Ag Education

In its third annual report, released in 1850, the University of Wisconsin Board of Regents recorded its interest in agricultural education:

> *The application of the sciences to the useful arts, including every industrial occupation which ministers to the well-being of society have become too numerous and too important to be neglected in any wisely constructed systems of general education.*
>
> *In this department of applied sciences, none of the industrial processes are more interesting than that of agriculture.*
>
> *This conviction is fast taking hold of the public mind in Europe and the older states of this Union, that for the acquisition of this valuable agricultural knowledge, it will not do to depend on the influences of popular Lectures and Addresses nor yet on the mass of floating information place before the Farmer through the agency of the Periodical Press.*
>
> *These views are rational and just, Agriculture Science, like all other sciences can only be acquired by study and research. The discipline of the school is essential to its acquisition. Without it, the farming processes fall to the low level of routine and drudgery. With it, Agriculture rises to the dignity of a profession, and indicates its undoubted claim to stand not only in the front rank of the experimental arts, but side by side with the learned professions in interest and honor as well as in profit.*[8]

# Summer in Wisconsin

This description of farm life helped earn author Hamlin Garland the Pulitzer Prize for his story *Rose of Dutcher's Coolly*, published in 1921:

> *It was full summer when we got back to Wisconsin, and The Old Homestead was at its best. The garden was red*

*with ripening fruit, the trees thick with shining leaves, and the thrushes and catbirds were singing in quiet joy. In the fields, the growing corn was sown its ordered spears, and the wheat was beginning to wave in the gentle wind. No land could be more hospitable, more abounding or more peaceful than our valley.*[9]

# EXPERIMENTAL FARM ESTABLISHED

Wisconsin's "experimental farms" are now called agricultural research stations. But their mission is still the same as when first established decades ago. They remain valuable outdoor laboratories and open-air classrooms used for studying the biological, agricultural and social sciences and natural resources:

*Through the liberality of the citizens of Dane County, an experimental farm has been secured at an expense of $40,000. The land purchased adjoined the University grounds, lying west of Mary Street, now Charter Street, and north of Sauk Road, now University Avenue...Application has been made to the proper authorities for the vacation of the streets intersecting the town lots purchases, which will undoubtedly be granted. The University grounds proper, heretofore belonging to the institution, contain 40 and 63–100 acres; they are contiguous to the above-described piece and with it form one tract with an area of over 235 acres.*[10]

# BARN RAISING

*A new dairy barn was built in 1898 by the University of Wisconsin's College of Agriculture. Professor F.H. King, who taught agricultural physics at the university, and farm superintendent Adams toured the States and Canada to get*

The Land

Dairy barn at the University of Wisconsin College of Agriculture and Life Sciences, 1908. *Courtesy of the University of Wisconsin–Madison Archives, no. S07291.*

*ideas on the structure and how it would function. Architect J.T.W. Jennings of Chicago was selected to design the building, which he fashioned after country barns found in Normandy. The interior furnishings were developed by Caryle and Adams.*

*The barn had a basement and three floors, plus a silo which was topped by a water tank. A ramp up to the third floor allowed feed and corn stalks to be hauled there for storage and silage. The feed could be dropped down to the cows stabled on the floor below. The silage cutter, feed grinder and other equipment were powered by a ten-horsepower electric motor placed on a small truck which ran on an iron track. This allowed it to be shifted around as needed.*

*There was room on the main floor for thirty-six cows, with eighteen on a side, with the cows facing each other. The center passage was ten feet wide to permit a team to drive through for green feeding.*

17

*The barn was eighty feet long by fifty feet wide, with two wings, each seventy feet long projecting at right angles to the end of the main building. A classroom, seventy by forty feet, was located between the wings. The right wing was designed for young stock and bulls while the left wing was for milking cows. Mangers for the milking cows were used for both feeding and watering. They were sloped toward the center with a drain valve hooked to the sewer. Water could be run in from a pipe at each end and drained after the cows finished drinking. The new barn cost around $16,000, with an additional $2,000 for equipment. Two flanking barns were added later to the complex.[11]*

## WORKING FARM PROVIDED REFLECTIVE TIME

In his delightful book about growing up on a small dairy farm near Janesville, *Any Damn Fool Can Be a Farmer*, author Bob Knopes described what rural life was like during the Great Depression:

*Farm life was a quiet life. Except for the steady drone of tractors during the day and the sounds of animals and insects at night, there was silence. Few cars came down our dirt road—four or five on the busiest day, and that included the mailman in the morning and the guy who threw the tightly wrapped Janesville Gazette into our driveway in the afternoon. In summer, our neighbors, the Liptows, whose rented farm was too small to devote any land to pasture, let their cattle graze along the road without fear of cars and trucks coming by. There was so little traffic that I yelled, "Here comes a car!" any time I saw a rooster-plume of dust moving along our road. I would stop what I was doing to follow its progress, hoping it would turn into our driveway.[12]*

Summertime washing hangs out to dry on a hilly Wisconsin family farm as a herd of dairy cattle lazily graze nearby. *Courtesy of Jim Brozek.*

## "FARM FOR SALE" NOTICE

Shrewd buyers could always get deals on animals and implements whenever a farm was sold, as evidenced by this newspaper notice from 1949:

> *Farm Loan Service Sale. Registered Holstein Dispersal Sale 95 Head of all Registered Holstein Cattle*
>
> *Frank Tillotson and A.D. Faville Estate, Lake Mills Wisconsin*
>
> *Location: 3 miles north of Lake Mills on County Trunk G. First farm north of Faville Grade School. Follow the arrows.*
>
> *One of the oldest established registered Holstein herds in this section of the state to be dispersed. Herd was formed by Mr. S.W. Faville about the year 1900, using foundation stock from Longfield, Dekel and Homestead bloodlines. Many good herds in this area were started with animals bought from the Faville herd.*[13]

## HEAVY WORKLOAD

In a report to the University of Wisconsin Board of Regents in 1904, College of Agriculture dean William Henry lamented the demands placed on his staff:

> *Instruction to Graduate, Long, Short, Dairy, and Farmers' Courses students, the heavy correspondence, the personal attention given to the thousands of visitors, the presence of our workers as expert stock judges at state and county fairs, lectures at teachers' meetings and Farmers' Institutes, and attendance on various agricultural gathering in our own State and elsewhere have all combined to encroach upon the time and resources of our small force of investigators to such a degree that we are doing far less research work than formerly. This matter weighs heavily on my*

*mind and discourages me more than you can know. I cannot ask my co-workers to do two things at once, or otherwise accomplish the impossible.*[14]

# FARM TALK

In 1923, the University of Wisconsin College of Agriculture agreed that meetings of farmers to discuss common issues were beneficial:

*Without question, state agricultural interests have been largely benefited by their sectional meeting of farmers. At these gatherings, the farmers meet each other to exchange views and experiences, also to get pointers and suggestions from those assigned to this service and the result is the dissemination of much useful, practical and valuable information; thereby stimulating and encouraging better methods in agricultural operations and accounting for much of the actual progress made by Badger farmers during recent years.*[15]

Workers and professors from the University of Wisconsin's College of Agriculture and Life Sciences study plants in an experimental garden in the 1920s. *Courtesy of the University of Wisconsin–Madison Archives, no. SO7783.*

# WHAT IT ALL MEANS

In their epic tale of Wisconsin from settlement to the present, *My Land, My Home My Wisconsin*, author Robert Gard and his wife, Maryo, related what land means to those who cultivate the soil:

> *Ours is the homeplace. I think about that so often; what it means to have a homeplace, and how all the ties to family and friends are there. The land is ours, it has our blood and the blood of all our people. My children feel the affinity of the land so deeply. They come home, to the homeplace. It is our farm. I feel a deep, deep bind between me and the land. I feel it every time I walk out across the fields. Like my ancestor, I want to shout out: This is mine! This is my land! My farm! I know I can never understand the whole story I wish I could, and the years of struggle, the years of change…How can I know of them, really?*[16]

# IT'S TIME TO PUT DOWN ROOTS

Ron Johnson, who has written about farms and farmers for more than thirty years, finally settled down in Crawford County. Previously, he lived in more places in Wisconsin that he cared to count, covering eleven counties: Vernon, Richland, Crawford (twice), Dane (twice), Shawano (twice), Wood, Clark, Waupaca, Columbia, Jefferson and Portage, plus living for a time as youngster in Indiana. He jokingly blamed his father, Carl Gunnar Johnson, for all that wandering.

Born in 1899, the elder Jonsson (as the name was originally spelled) immigrated to the United States from Sweden when he turned twenty-one, living in New York City in 1924 and then in New Jersey and Chicago before the Great Depression. During the economic crunch, the elder Johnson lost his construction business, his cottage along the Fox River and some property near downtown Chicago.

In a column in *Dairy Star*, a midwestern newspaper devoted to dairy farming, his son related his own life journey:

Carl Gunnar Jonsson (right) and his pal Emil Axelson ride their bicycles in Sweden in 1919. Jonsson was born in 1899, came to the United States in about 1924 and raised dairy and beef cattle in Wisconsin. He was the father of farm columnist Ron Johnson. *Courtesy of Ron Johnson.*

*With $500 and a pickup truck, he* [Johnson's father] *moved out of the city and rented a dairy farm in northeastern Illinois. A couple of years later, he bought a dairy farm nearby, in northwest Indiana.*

*After too many heartaches there—the drowning of his first son in a cattle water tank, and the death of his first wife—Dad packed us up and left for southwest Wisconsin. I was the youngest of that tribe that included my parents and eight brothers and sisters.*

*We stayed on that 809-acre, 60-cow dairy farm until 1961. Then it was off to a 100-acre farm near Richland Center, where my dad somewhat retired and fretted over his beef cattle.*

*In 1966, it was time to move again, this time to a 120-acre ridge-and-valley farm in Crawford County, again to raise beef cattle. My father had tired of the Richland Center place partly because of his constant battles with Ash Creek. That stubborn stream tore out the bridge to the back fields and pastures almost as fast as my father could stubbornly rebuild it. Concrete piers and steel I-beams did nothing to deter that flooding creek.*

*But in Crawford County, near Seneca, small Copper Creek wound its way far down in a narrow, wooded valley, below and away from any fields and pastures…*

*But, for years before moving back here—back "home"—as I think of it, I longed to return. I have the Mississippi River a few miles to my west. The Wisconsin River flows just six miles away, near the small community of Wauzeka. The home farm near Seneca is still there, although the only two recognizable things remaining are the land itself and the windmill. The windmill seems small and lonely now.*

*My wife, Jessica, and I just bought a house on nine Crawford County acres…We and our four house cats and two dogs are digging in, hoping to never move, ever, ever again.*

*One of my greatest pleasures each day is to trudge up our tenth-of-a-mile-long driveway to collect the mail. On the return trip, heading down the hill, I have laid out before me a vast panorama of Crawford County hillsides and ridgetop. The land has many trees, and barns, houses, silos and fields are spread out before my gaze.*

*Best of all, as I hear the crunch of gravel under my feet, I realize that his small patch of land is home and it is mine. I pray that it proves to be a place of fertile ground, well watered, where I can, at long last, put down roots.*[17]

## CASH BY THE BUSHEL

This notice in a 1923 newsletter for the staff of the University of Wisconsin College of Agriculture alerted them to a much-appreciated donation to help with agricultural education:

*According to the will of Dr. Calvin K. Jayne of Madison in 1923, a sum of money to be known as "Cora I. Jayne Agricultural Student Fund" is to become available as a loan fund for students from Wisconsin in the College of Agriculture upon the final settlement of the estate, amounting to approximately*

Farmworkers cultivate crops at the University of Wisconsin in the 1930s. *Courtesy of the University of Wisconsin–Madison Archives, no. SO7784.*

*$70,000. If the income from this money, after certain payments are made to certain heirs, is not required for a loan fund, it can be made available for scholarships at the discretion of the Board of Regents.*[18]

## FOUNDING OF THE WISCONSIN FARM BUREAU

In 1920, Wisconsin farmers in eight counties needed to organize themselves for the betterment of their businesses. In that year, representatives of farmers in Rock County met with J.C. Sailor of the Illinois Farm Bureau to discuss ways of taking action to protect their livelihood. "Farmers are skeptical because so many unworthy organizations grow up, but it is up to the farm bureau to show the farmers of their sincerity. Agriculture is the foundation of everything. We have let other people attend to our business long enough," he told them.

Within a year, farmers were organizing not only in Rock County but also in Fond du Lac, Waukesha, Jefferson, Walworth, Dodge, Dane, Ozaukee and Crawford Counties. They held a statewide meeting in Waukesha on May 27, 1920, to approve affiliation with the American Farm Bureau Federation, becoming the thirty-second state farm bureau to align themselves with the national group. The first president of the Wisconsin bureau was George Hull of Whitewater, who served in 1921 and from 1923 to 1924.

In those early days, the farm bureau worked on such issues as rural electrification, group purchasing of farm supplies and marketing of farm commodities and insurance. Farm bureau leaders recognized the need to provide automobile coverage to members who were often unable to find affordable insurance since farmers were considered extremely high risk. Subsequently, the Farm Bureau Mutual Insurance Company of Wisconsin was formed in 1934. That company evolved into what is now the Rural Mutual Insurance Company.

*Acting as individuals, farmers have comparatively little influence. Acting together in the best interests of the nation, they are a powerful force…Like the school and church, farm organizations are an accepted part of our way of living. We take them very much for granted…They have been elevated to the position of a commonplace institution. Commonplace institutions are likely to be our most important and at the same time the least impressive.*

*One seldom misses them until they fail to function properly, or are gone…Farmers can only be served by organizations which are made up of farm people, led by farm leaders, financed entirely by farmers and run in the interests of the men and women on the farm who appreciate that the farmers' interests are best served when society as a whole is best served.*[19]

## Value of United States Agriculture

Speaking in 1967 at the University of Illinois Centennial Symposium on the Land Grant University and World Food Needs, Dean Glenn S. Pound of the University of Wisconsin's College of Agriculture and Life Sciences spoke eloquently on the importance of United States agriculture. He started his lecture by quoting Isaiah 51:1—"Look to the rock from which you were hewn and to the quarry from which you were digged."

*I begin this paper with the above quotation from Isaiah to emphasize that much of America's greatness came from agriculture. By steadily increasing efficiency, it provided a pool of labor for industrialization; by using in turn, the technology of industry, it has given the United States man's greatest food affluence. It is, perhaps, our greatest tool in international diplomacy. It is appropriate, therefore, in a centennial celebration of this great public university which lies in the heart of America's bread basket, that we look at our agriculture with an eye to its future role. Just as agriculture has dictated much of our national development, so will it be the strongest determinant of our future.*[20]

# A FARMER'S WORDS TO LIVE BY

*Knowledge of production alone may make a man a slave.*
*Knowledge of distribution alone may make a man a plutocrat.*
*Knowledge of consumption alone may make a man a parasite.*
*Knowledge of all three makes a man an effective citizen of democracy.*[21]

# THE COULEE FARM

Author Hamlin Garland, in his autobiographical *A Son of the Middle Border*, touches on the beauty and roughness of the Wisconsin frontier:

> *Our farm lay well up in what is called Green's coulee, in a little valley just over the road which runs along the La Crosse river in western Wisconsin. It contained one hundred and sixty acres of land which crumpled against the wooded hills on the east and lay well upon a ridge to the west. Only two families lived above us, over the height to the north was the land of the red people, and small bands of their hunters used occasionally to come trailing down across our meadow on their way to and from La Crosse, which was their immemorial trading point.*
>
> *Sometimes they walked into our house, always without knocking—but then we understood their ways. No one knocks at the wigwam of a red neighbor, and we were not afraid of them, for they were friendly, and our mother often gave them bread and meat which they took (always without thanks) and ate with much relish while sitting beside our fire. All this seemed very curious to us, but as they were accustomed to share their food and lodging with one another so they accepted my mother's bounty in the same matter-of-fact fashion.*[22]

## Show Me the Money

The first legislative appropriation of $5,000 to the University of Wisconsin College of Agriculture and Life Sciences (CALS) for the establishment of Farmers' Institutes came in 1885. By 1887, the legislature increased the amount to $12,000, and Farmers' Institutes attracted fifty-thousand people in three hundred sessions statewide. During the first twenty years of the institutes, Wisconsin progressed from a poor, single-grain state to a leader in dairying and diversified farming. The economic consequences were seen across the state. At Beaver Dam, thirty-eight cooperative creameries and cheese factories were formed by institute attendees. Within seven years, they paid Dodge County farmers more than $500,000 annually.[23]

## Move Over!

Wisconsin legislators had no love of motorcars when the "devil wagons" first appeared on the state roads. Under laws drawn up in the early 1900s, the driver of an automobile had to slow up when meeting a horse-drawn rig. If the horses or driver were frightened, the car operator had to stop and allow the team to be led past the vehicle. An early motorist in Fond du Lac County recalled one occasion when he slowed down to comply with the law and met a farm couple on a rural road. He called out to the farmer and wife to see if they needed any help with the snorting horses. The man replied that he could manage the team all right but that "the Old Lady is pretty skittish."[24]

## Join the Gang

In 1888, several organizations represented Wisconsin farmers. Among them were the Wisconsin State Agricultural Society, State Dairymen's Association, Shorthorn Breeders' Association, State

There is always a special relationship between a farmer and his hardworking draft horse. *Courtesy of Jim Brozek.*

Sheep Breeders and Growers' Association and the Southeast Sheep Breeders' and Wool Growers' Association.[25]

The first dairymen's association was a loose assembly of area farmers founded in Fond du Lac County in January 13, 1870, making it the first such group for the industry in the state. The larger, more organized Wisconsin Dairymen's Association was launched in Watertown on February 15, 1872. The group was instrumental in establishing uniform measurements and quality standards for the state's cheese industry and in marketing it collectively to ensure a good price. Members were able to get the railroads to offer speedy service and use refrigerated freight cars as early as 1871.[26]

## LAND GRANT SYSTEM

The College of Agriculture and Life Sciences (CALS) fulfills the UW–Madison's mission as a land-grant university. This dates back to 1862, when Congress established a network of colleges devoted to agriculture and mechanics. This was known as the "land grant" system because each state received an allotment of federal land to pay for its new school. Wisconsin received 240,000 acres and sold them for $1.25 each. The state legislature opted to direct those funds to the new University of Wisconsin in Madison to carry out the land-grant mission.

While the College itself wasn't officially established until 1889, the seeds were planted several decades earlier. In the 1870s, the university used $40,000 donated by Dane County to purchase a farm west of campus and established a department of agriculture. In 1880, it hired W.A. Henry, who over the next seventeen years would take the lead in creating and molding the programs that make up the CALS of today.

Agricultural chemist Stephen Moulton Babcock is known for inventing a test for measuring the butterfat content in milk, as well as for the single-grain experiment, which led to the development of the field of nutritional science.

In 1883, the legislature established the Wisconsin Agricultural Experiment Station. This was the foundation for today's world-renowned research program. In 1885, the university began offering a winter course for farmers, a program that continues today as the Farm and Industry Short Course. The same year saw the beginning of a program called the Farmers' Institutes, a sort of traveling school of agriculture for farmers that met at various locations around the state. This was a precursor to today's Cooperative Extension and other outreach programs. In 1889, the university put all of these agricultural offerings under a new College of Agriculture, with Henry as dean.

The college has evolved and grown over the decades to reflect changes in the fabric of society and in the areas of knowledge that it studies. Practical studies related to crop and livestock production and farm life gradually delved deeper as scientists strove to understand the underlying biological processes. Today, the college generates new knowledge about agriculture, natural resource management and protection, human health and nutrition, community development and related topics. Faculty and staff in nineteen academic departments and a number of interdisciplinary programs carry out these lines of study.[27]

## IT'S ALL IN A NAME

In 1930, the Wisconsin Farm Bureau finally got its own publication for distribution to members. Edited by E.E. Schroeder, the magazine immediately became a popular tool for getting out the word on the organization's activities. Initially, though, it did not have an official name. To remedy the situation, the bureau's board held a competition to name the tabloid, with the winner receiving a ten-dollar gold piece. That lure was enough to draw a flood of submissions, since it was during the Great Depression and farmers everywhere were financially hurting.

The board finally selected *Badger Farm Bureau News*, as suggested by Clara Thoreson of Chilton. The *News* was the regular bureau publication from 1930 to 1986, when the bimonthly magazine *AgVenture* was launched. *Frontline*, a monthly newsletter, was added in 1994 to complement *AgVenture*.[28]

## CHANGE IN THE AIR

In his essay "With One Foot in the Furrow: A Perspective for the Future," Christen D. Upper of the Department of Plant Pathology at University of Wisconsin–Madison discussed how the agricultural world was changing:

> *There are, however, external forces sufficient to cause us to change. First, our society, our university, and the agriculture of our state change. The plowman drives a tractor today, he does not walk in the furrow behind the plow. Nor can we expect him to. If we don't assure that our organization and personnel are able to serve these changing institutions the social, education and economic interests of the state may (rightly) inquire about the justification for our existence.*
>
> *Secondly, our science changes. (An optimist might say it progresses). And knowledge developed in other disciplines becomes available to plant pathology. How can be we perceive of ourselves as leaders of others are the first to endorse each fad? Thus, changes—perceived or real—in and around the field of plant pathology provide substantial force toward reshaping our view of where we should be and what we should become.[29]*

## VALUE OF EDUCATION

A Portage County farmer eagerly described how the University of Wisconsin's short course in agriculture changed his world:

> *There were fourteen kids in our family and I was the oldest. We all worked. Hard. And we never got away much, and didn't get*

*to any parties or such. But we were happy. My folks went to a dance once in a while in the neighborhood, but we kids didn't get to go. I started to milk cows when I was seven years old, milked right out in the cow yard. I was kicked plenty of times, and you had to watch out for the cow's tail, in bur time, and in the fields I drove the team and picked up stones. Then when the day's work was done I had to go in the house and work. I used to have to haul the milk two miles to the creamery, and then drive the team back and put them in the barn and then walk back the two miles to school. I sure did want an education; the Short Course at the agriculture college, available to boys like me, opened up my whole life for me.[30]*

# DAIRY INDUSTRY NEWS WRAPUP, 1914

*Arcadia*—The new creamery of the Glencoe Cooperative Creamery Co., will be completed by October.

*Crandon*—The Crandon Creamery Co has been incorporated, with the capital of $5,000, by J.M. Whisant and others.

*Columbus*—Edward and Ralph Montgomery have exchanged their creamery here for the Grell Creamery in Neillsville.

*Eagle River*—A committee headed by Mart Hizel has charge of building for the new creamery. The farmers have subscribed for $5,800 worth of stock.

*Egg Harbor*—Max Wilson is promoting new creamery projects.

*Haywood*—There has been incorporated the Haywood Creamery Association, with a capital of $5,000, by Ole Hanson.

*Hillsboro*—N.B. Lee and others have formed the Hillsboro Creamery Co., with a capital of $5,000.

*Middleton—Hopkins Brothers have sold their creamery to C. Henning.*

*Ogdensburg—J.R. Parmenter and others have organized the Ogdensburg Cooperate Co., with a capital of $12,000.*

*Ruplinger—The creamery has been bought by farmers and will be operated on the cooperative plan.*

*Stevens Point—Ellis Creamery Co. has been incorporated, with a capital of $2,400.*[31]

## THE RETURN OF THE PRIVATE

With the outbreak of the American Civil War, Wisconsin raised 91,379 soldiers for the Union army, organized into fifty-three infantry regiments, four cavalry regiments, a company of Berdan's sharpshooters, thirteen light artillery batteries and one unit of heavy artillery. Most served in the Western Theater, although several regiments served in Eastern armies, including three regiments within the famed Iron Brigade. Of those in service, 3,794 were killed in action or mortally wounded, 8,022 died of disease and 400 were killed in accidents.

The total mortality was 12,216 men, about 13.4 percent of total enlistments. About 1 in 9 residents served in the military. Many were farmers, recently arrived immigrants who left their fields to battle for their adopted nation. Wisconsin author Hamlin Garland poignantly wrote of the return of these men to their farm homes after the war:

> *The nearer the train drew toward La Crosse, the soberer the little group of "vets" became. On the long way from New Orleans, they had beguiled tedium with jokes and friendly chaff; or with planning with elaborate detail what they were going to do now, after the war. A long journey, slowly, irregularly, yet persistently pushing northward. When they entered Wisconsin territory, they*

*gave a cheer, and another when they reached Madison, but after they sank into a dumb expectancy. Comrades dropped off one or two points beyond, until there were only four or five left who were bound for La Crosse County.*

*Three of them were gaunt and brown, the fourth was gaunt and pale, with signs of fever and ague upon him. One had a great scar down his temple, one limped, and they all had unnaturally large, bright eyes, showing emaciation. There were no bands greeting them at the station, no banks of gayly dressed ladies waving handkerchiefs and shouting, "Bravo!" as they came in on the caboose of a freight train into the towns that had cheered and blared them on their way to war. As they looked out or stepped upon the platform for a moment, while the train stood at the station, the loafers looked at them indifferently. Their blue coats, dusty and grimy, were too familiar now to excite notice, much less a friendly word. They were the last of the army to return, and the loafers were surfeited with such sights.*

*The train chugged forward so slowly that it seemed to be midnight before they should reach La Crosse. The little squad grumbled and swore, but it was no use; the train would not hurry, and, as a matter of fact, it was nearly two o'clock when the engine whistled "down brakes."*

*All of the group were farmers, living in districts several miles out of the town, and all were poor.*[32]

# THE AUCTION

In an essay published in the *Eau Claire Leader Telegram* in 1999, Cynthia Hofacker of Eau Claire remembers the selling of her family's farm:

*The yard was muddy. A late winter snowstorm had blanketed the farmyard with six inches of wet, sloppy snow. It seemed only fitting. The farm looked old, weathered…*

*It had taken Dad more than 35 years to accumulate his animals, machinery, and tools, and in less than eight hours, everything would be gone. I didn't remember his tools looking so rusted before. Was that the "good" Leland tractor? When did it lose its bright blue paint?...*

*Dad looks tired. The farm accident last summer had taken a lot out of him. We almost lost him that day. The creditors are calling...Dad and Mom are making the right decision. We're all here. All seven children, their spouses and grandchildren have come from throughout the state.*

*"The auctioneer is ready to begin.*[33]

# UNREST HITS 1930S WISCONSIN FARM SECTOR

The agriculture sector was not immune to the troubles during the Great Depression, as banks foreclosed on farms. The militant Wisconsin Milk Pool in the Fox River Valley called for milk strikes in February and May 1933. But the larger Farm Holiday Association and Wisconsin Agricultural Council refused to join in the strike, and violence resulted. Two men were killed in the May strike as dairy farmers dumped milk into ditches and rival groups clashed. Governor Albert Schmedeman called out the state militia to restore order.

One striker in Clark County recalled:

*With every highway leading into this city blocked by determined pickets of the milk strikers, Neillsville this week found itself virtually cut off from the outside world so far as farm products are concerned. A similar situation exists in other parts of the county and nearby counties, it is reported, while in some localities the blockade has not as yet got under way. Milk plants in this city and elsewhere remained idle as the flow of milk was effectively cut off...*

*How long the strike will be carried on is not known. None of the pickets or men back of the movement can venture a guess as to the duration period, but are unanimous in declaring that it must be carried on until agriculture is placed upon an equality with industry. "We will suffer a loss in this strike," said a farmer at the meeting Tuesday night, "but we have reached the point where we are in a desperate situation and we must sacrifice now in the hopes that our condition will be improved. We can't go on under our present circumstances."[34]*

# FAIR OPENS WITH FLAIR

Fairs had been held in Brown County since 1877, first with the Brown County Horticultural Society, which lasted until 1889, and then the Oneida Fair Association, which held events in Oneida until 1908. The contemporary Brown County Fair officially kicked off September 1–3, 1909, following the formation of a nonprofit association to manage the operation. It featured acrobats, balloon races and "enormous sums to be awarded" to winners of exhibits, as well as showcases of farm animals and products:

*The big Brown County Fair was opened yesterday in a blaze of glory, and today the fair is on in full bloom…new buildings have been constructed, old ones repaired and repainted, the race track lengthened and improved, and the grandstand enlarged.*

*The cattle exhibit is without a doubt the finest that can be seen in any part of the state. There is a good exhibit of all kinds of farm implements and gasoline engines to be seen in the center of the race track.[35]*

# The People

*The shiftless, lazy, careless farmer need not expect to be successful for he will make a miserable failure if he tried. It needs brains; it needs untiring energy and above all it needs men who can adapt themselves to circumstances and learn and profit by experience.*
*—F.W. Coon, 1885[1]*

## NATIVE AMERICAN FARMERS

Tilling the soil was nothing new to what would become the state of Wisconsin. Prehistoric people and more contemporary Native American farmers were skilled in caring for the land. Research shows that cultivation of the soil was a prime occupation at least as early as AD 1000 in the Chippewa River Valley. Corn, squash and beans were the "three sisters," grown on the same mound to keep down weeds, replenish the soil and retain water.

The crops augmented the wild herbs, fruits and game that made up diets in those days long ago. Woodland villages, sometimes numbering more than two hundred persons, were established throughout "Wisconsin." These were not permanent settlements, since the residents regularly moved to follow the migration of animals and fowl. But when they did locate at a site, land around the encampments was cleared, usually by burning brush. Some fields were as large as one hundred acres.

The Ojibwes, who came to northern Wisconsin from further east in the 1700s, not only harvested wild rice but also planted and cared for this staple. Native planters told ethnologists such as Albert E. Jenks that, generally, the rice was sown in an easterly direction from one body of water to the next until it reached every Ojibwe community. Early records indicated that rice was gathered from Red Cedar Lake to seed Lake Chetek, Rice Lake, Bear Lake, Moose-Ear Lake and backwaters along the Lac Courte Oreilles River. The latter was seeded in the early 1860s, after an 1854 treaty established reservation borders.

By 1900, white farmers were planting rice and building processing plants to serve a growing demand for the product throughout the States.[2]

# NOT EXACTLY PLYMOUTH ROCK

Like the Pilgrims of Plymouth, French traders Pierre Esprit Radisson and his brother-in-law, the Sieur de Groseilliers, nearly starved to death their first winter in Wisconsin. Wandering the frozen Northwoods, Radisson and Groseilliers struggled to find food, eventually resorting to eating their two dogs before finding some Ottawas living in a camp along headwaters of the Chippewa River. Living with the Indians for part of the winter, Radisson and Groseilliers were given wild rice and duck and other fowl (including wild turkey). In his memoirs, Groseilliers said that he even gave a speech of thanksgiving at one meal. While not exactly the feast enjoyed in Plymouth in the fall of 1621, the Ottawas saved Radisson and Groseilliers from probable death.[3]

## Black Farmers in Wisconsin

After World War II, the movement of African Americans from the rural South to urban locations became a torrent, but for those blacks who wanted to farm, the "Cut-Over" was the kind of place to try. Echoing the efforts of the black community in the town of Hoard in Clark County in the 1930s and 1940s, African American Dan Blakey farmed near Gromton in Clark County in the 1990s. Blakey, who grew up on a farm in Minnesota, struggled to hold on to several central Wisconsin farms before a white widow, Ruth Searls, offered to make him a partner and let him take over her farm. From his share of the farm's income, Blakey had bought the farm's herd and machinery in two years.[4]

## Tough Row to Hoe

Palmer Gardner was the first settler in Spring Prairie, Walworth County, coming there from Onondaga County, New York, in early April 1836. He started building his log house on April 15, 1836, and was living on the same farm as late as 1869. The following letter was sent from Milwaukee to Dr. E.H. Porter in Skaneatels, Onondaga County, and dated February 16, 1837. Other letters Gardner sent to friends and relatives over the next months were addressed from "Milwaukie." Punctuation, grammar and spelling from this letter have been adapted to today's norms:

> On preparing to write to you, the first Idea that presents itself is, that you had a right to expect a letter from me long before this, but if I now give you a history of my…year past you will be in possession of the whole facts at once. Last March 1, I started (out) for this place with $2,200 (in my wallet).
>
> My expenses since have been traveling here (are) $100 paid for labor; $300 paid for provisions; $600 for a team; $400, incidental expenses to mechanics; and $500 for other. Amounting in all to $1,900. Charged against my farm for which I have to

*show (for my labors this past year): 100 bushels of potatoes, 70
acres ploughed, 30 acres fenced, one log house, two yoke of oxen,
one wagon, one horse. It will cost me yet $400 more to live and
(to) till my farm until I expect returns next harvest.*

*Last year, I sowed eight (acres) to oats (and) three to potatoes.
The grubs eat up the corn. The oats turned out 100 bushels; the
potatoes, 200 bushels. But I shall put in 70 acres next spring and
hope for good crops—I am trying this winter, in addition to my
ploughed field, to get a pasture of 200 acres fenced.*

*The first six months, I lived mostly without a floor in my
house or a Woman to cook but at commencement of winter we
got better prepared for living and now have things as comfortable
as our Neighbors.*[5]

# NORWEGIAN ÉMIGRÉS

Three weeks after they were married, Lars Anderson, twenty-
seven, and his new bride, twenty-two-year-old Grethe (Paulson)
Anderson, left Christiana, Norway (now Oslo), and sailed to
America. They were joined by Lars's younger brother, Jens. The
date was April 20, 1853.

The Andersons spent seven weeks at sea, arriving in New York
on June 7, among the six thousand other Norwegians who left
their home country that year for North America. They traveled
to Milwaukee by lake steamer and walked to Waupun, about fifty
miles to the northeast. The couple stayed in that area for some
three years, getting to know the ways of America and their new
language, English. In 1856, accompanied by their year-old son Carl,
the Andersons travel by foot and covered wagon from Waupun to
Eau Claire. They settled on 120 brushy acres in Chippewa Falls
Township, with access to water from Big Elk Creek. Anderson's
brother Jens claimed an adjacent tract of land.

Stumps were cleared by hand and then burned, with the soil
broken by plow and smoothed by pulling logs over the uneven
ground. The first year, they planted root vegetables, and Lars and

Lewis and Greta Anderson. *Courtesy of the Chippewa Valley Historical Society.*

Jens hunted for meat, bringing in enough to survive the next winter. Gradually, the farm took shape, and the family was able to move into a larger house. The Andersons eventually purchased milk cows, a team of horses, sheep, hogs and chickens, thus becoming "successful." They raised wheat, corn, oats and potatoes, as well as made butter and cut timber.

Tax records showed that the Andersons gradually became Anglicized, with Lars becoming "Lewis" and Grethe becoming "Greta." They lived on their farm for the rest of their lives, raising ten children, four of whom died as youngsters. Throughout those years, Larson was active in the community, serving as constable, justice of the peace and town supervisor.[6]

## ALL IS WELL WITH THE WORLD

*Health, strength, competence, and peace attend upon on the farmer's toil. The sun and the sky smile directly upon his head. The fruits and the flowers of the earth spring beneath his feet, obedient to his call. The fresh breezes fill his lungs and fan his manly brow. His condition is one of practical independence. He sits beneath his own vine and fig tree.*

*He eats the fruit of his own labor. His health and his honors depend not upon the smiles of princes or the favor of the populace, but upon his own right arm, and the blessing of that God who has set his bow in the Heavens, as a witness that summer and winter, seed-time and harvest shall not fail.*

*Among the ten thousand means which art has devised, for improving the condition of the human family, the enlightened pursuits of Agriculture still remain the most inviting, the most productive, the employment of the great mass of mankind; whatever lightens its burdens or elevates its votaries, must command the ready attention of all right-minded persons.*

*The Wisconsin Farmer should honor and love his calling. It is the occupation of primeval innocence. The purest and greatest of men have turned to it, when the world's wealth and honors and stations palled upon their cloyed senses.*[7]

# GRANDPA RUSSELL TELLS HIS STORY

Irish emigrant Patrick Russell, who dictated these notes, eventually moved to Iowa in 1870 and purchased a 160-acre farm near Fredericksburg where "we heard the wolves howl around the log house." He died surrounded by family on February 2, 1917.

*This is to certify that the following is the correct story of my life as I remember it and I desire that the history be written while I am yet here to verify same and hear it read. This is the ninety-second year of my life and thanks to a divine providence I am still in the full possession of my senses. While sitting in my comfortable chair surrounded by my beloved children and grandchildren, I take great pleasure in dictating the following bestowing my blessings on all my children to the Fourth Generation.*

*I was born in Templemore, County Cork, Ireland, March 16, 1825. Our family consisted to two sisters and three brothers, Joseph, William and Micheal. My earliest recollections are having spent a happy boyhood, up to the time my Mother died. When I was fourteen of age, my father brought us to America. We sailed on the Tyrene, by Capt. Allocob. We landed at Quebec, then via the St. Lawrence to Montreal.*

*The English had sheds built along the shore for the comfort of incoming passengers. English agents there wanted my father to go into Canada to take up land and offered us a yoke of oxen and a year's provisions, besides a quarter section of land for each of us boys, but my father said, "No." I cannot agree to that. I have living long enough under the English government and now that I am so near to free America, there I will go.*

*From Montreal, we came down the St. Lawrence River thro Lake Erie to Buffalo, thence by boat thro the Lakes to Milwaukee. There we were met by our uncle Jim Lynch. He had been in Boston a few years ahead of us. My father had written to him to get us a piece of land somewhere in the West. He came to Milwaukee, then a small village on Lake Michigan. He had bought us a small family farm in Washington County thirty miles Northwest of Milwaukee. He had been there the previous winter and with his companions had cleared eighty acres in anticipation of our coming. There were no other people within ten miles of us. My sister, seven-years-old, and two other women were the only females in the whole Township. Before leaving Milwaukee, we bought two cows which we drove out.*

*Lynch and friends had built us a small log house, thatched with the bark of trees. We arrived in June. We had brought a few sacks of potatoes from Milwaukee which we planted in holes dug in the ground with four spades we had brought from Ireland. The spades were the only implements in the entire section. We had an abundant crop.*

*Our neighbors later were the two Mountains, "Big Billie" and "Little Bill," Jim Murphy, Andy O'Brien, Tom Mangin and Tim Garvey. This was in "Town Nine," Merton was the nearest town, ten miles away.*

*I married when I was twenty-eight years old to Mary Martin on Easter Sunday, March 23rd, 1857 by Rev. Fr. Hoobs* [in Hartford, Wisconsin].[8]

# SOLDIERS CELEBRATE WITH GRAND COOKING

The Iron Brigade was an infantry unit in the Union Army of the Potomac during the American Civil War, consisting of the Second, Sixth and Seventh Wisconsin Volunteer Infantry Regiments and units from Indiana and Michigan. The brigade was noted for its fighting ability and suffered the highest percentage of casualties of any brigade in the war. Many of the soldiers were drawn from Wisconsin's large farm population. The following is from a letter written around Thanksgiving 1861 by an officer in the Second Wisconsin Regiment, serving near Arlington, Virginia.

*Washington, November 29, 1861*

*Perhaps you think, because we are away from home, living in tents with nothing but tin cups and plates that we suffer from the want of the necessaries of Life. Now that you may not grieve away your life and flesh, I enclose you a Bill of Fare which we had to select from on Thanksgiving—yesterday. Gov. Randall was present at our table in our tent and ate off our tin dishes, drank champagne from our borrowed glasses and coffee from our tin cups. So was Gov. Seward, so was Senator Wilson, so was Gen. King and staff, some of Gen. McDowell's staff and sundry other distinguished officers and individuals too numerous to mention beside some who were not.*

*The President intended to come but was interrupted just at the time of starting. Golly! Weren't we proud of the day and the occasion and the dinner and company? So we ate and drank and talked and talked and drank and ate and sung and toasted and joked and joked and toasted and sung until the flesh which was weak gave out while the spirit was still willing. But the best of it was we adjourned in good season and departed in quietness and peace leaving the largest share of the eatables to the men and music and others who had assisted us. There were about fifty officers and guests at the table and as the Apostle says it was "A feast of reason and a flow of soul."*

*The bill of fare was as follows:*

*Soup*

*Oysters, Turkey with Jelly, Ducks, Spring Chickens, Lamb with Mint sauce, Sirloin beef, Pig, Wild Goose, Baked Beans, Boiled Ham, Corned Beef with Cabbage*

*Vegetables: Sweet Potatoes, Irish Potatoes, Onions, Celery*

*Entrees: Pork Chops with Fried Apple, Chicken Pie Yankee Style, Fried Liver, Mutton Chops, Beefsteak, Ham and Eggs, Lobster Salad, Scalloped Oysters*

*Bread: Corn Bread, Rye Bread, Wheat Bread*

*Relishes: French Mustard, Cole Slaw, Pickles, Horse Radish, Celery, Worcestershire Sauce*

*Pastry: Pumpkin Pie, Mince Pie, Ice Cream*

*Wines: Sparkling Catawba, Heidsick, Coffee and Tea*

The following is from a Thanksgiving letter from a soldier with the Seventh Regiment, also at Arlington on November 28, 1861:

*Messrs. Editors:*

*We beg the privilege to say a few words to our friends and relatives through the medium of your valuable paper. As today is Thanksgiving and as we are not compelled to drill, we have a little time to spare to write and feeling that our Annual feast day will be, this year, to many households an unusual solemn occasion, the empty chair telling a story of devotion, of courage, of determination to shield the remaining ones in the enjoyment of the blessings they are singing praises for and tenderly will the prayer ascend for the absent one's protection and guidance. We hope the day throughout the land will be observed as it never was observed before. A portion of the day might well be devoted to the preparation of a fitting tribute to our country's defenders.*

*Today the weather is fine; the sun shines bright and warm as at a June noonday. At half past eleven we, Gen. King's brigade, were assembled in front of the Lee mansion—Gen. King's headquarters—where His Excellency, Gov. Randall, addressed us. He spoke at some length, paid us many compliments and bade us farewell—yes, I fear a last farewell to many of us. We then returned to our quarters to partake of our noonday meal which, I may say, was almost a feast; and, as there is a good deal of doubt on the part of our friends at home as to our having enough to eat, I will mention the bill of fare which is not an uncommon thing with us; we seated ourselves at a pine table covered with a white muslin cloth.*

*After returning thanks to the Giver of All Good, the thought occurred to us whether our friends and loved ones at home had as good a dinner to eat—but I am digressing. We commenced with mashed potatoes, roast beef, warm biscuit, fresh butter, pickles, tea and cream, winding up with apple pie, sweet cakes and crackers, fresh peaches, plum sauce, tomato sauce, oysters, fried nut cakes, green apples and good sweet cider.*

*Considering that we are in the midst of enemies and in a soldier's tent almost on the field of battle, you may well imagine that, as it was all prepared by a sister's experienced hand who was seated at the head of the table, that it had a look of homelikeness…Let us hope and pray that when another Thanksgiving rolls about it may be such as one as will see our country rescued from its present dangers and that we will again be a united people joining in a general Thanksgiving to him who holds our destiny in his hands.[9]*

# GOOD OL' BOYS

A notice in the *Wisconsin Agriculturalist* newspaper of August 20, 1903, was entitled "Benefits of Green County":

*A prospective buyer of purebred live stock can find almost anything he wants in that line in Green County, Wisconsin. He can go there depending that if one breeder does not have what he wants, another will, and if he wants to buy, he will come home owning something. The trip will not only be one of business but also of pleasure, for Green County stockmen are right good fellows as well as businessmen.[10]*

# HENRY CULLEN ADAMS, PURE FOOD ADVOCATE

Wisconsin farmer Henry Cullen Adams became a United States congressman from the Dairy State and was a longtime advocate of pure food laws.

Born on November 28, 1850, Adams grew up on a farm in southern Wisconsin. He attended the University of Wisconsin–Madison but needed to drop out because of his health and never earned a degree. After marrying Anne Burkley Norton in 1878, he operated a successful dairy and fruit farm and served as president of the Wisconsin Dairymen's Association.

Adams was always interested in politics and felt that his experiences as a farmer would be helpful. He was elected to the Wisconsin State Assembly in 1883 and served until 1887, when he became a member of the Wisconsin Board of Agriculture (1887–95). Adams became Wisconsin superintendent of public property (1889–91) and food and dairy commissioner (1898–1902) under Governor W.D. Hoard, pushing for legislation advancing pure food regulations. He was also secretary of the Wisconsin Horticultural Society and president of the Wisconsin Dairymen's Association.

In 1902, Adams continued his legislative work, being elected to the United States House of Representatives from the Second District of Wisconsin. He was a progressive Republican and admirer of Robert M. La Follette Sr. Adams worked tirelessly for passage of the Meat Inspection Act and the Pure Food and Drug Act. However, he died of intestinal illness on July 9, 1906, in Chicago while traveling from Washington to his home in Wisconsin. He is buried at Madison's Forest Hill Cemetery in Section 17, Lot 003, Grave 1.[11]

# No Desire to Change

John Mills Smith came from Morristown, New Jersey, where some of his relatives fought in the Revolutionary War. Seeking adventure, he came to Wisconsin and settled near Green Bay in 1854. Working first as a timber scanner, able to look at a grove of trees and tell how many board feet it could produce, Smith was a frequent speaker at meetings of the Horticultural Society and regularly wrote for the organization's newsletters and reports. Smith and his wife had eight children, several of whom farmed with him.

He also served two hitches with the Union army during the Civil War (1861 and 1864). Smith and his eldest son, Henry, fought side by side in several engagements under Ulysses S. Grant. One of Smith's descendants was the famed sports commentator and Pulitzer Prize winner Walter (Red) Smith.

> *Why should I not be a horticulturist? I often wish that I was a much better one... The knowledge that we suppose we have about plant life and growth, is much of it very unsatisfactory. I can ask myself hundreds of questions in a day that I cannot answer.*
>
> *I know of no other profession in life that I could enter into with more energy and enthusiasm, than the one I am now in. Neither my wife nor myself have a desire, or any expectation of changing our business, until the good Father shall call us home, and as we trust, will place us in a garden much fairer than any ever made by human hands.*[12]

## ROSE OF DUTCHER'S COOLLY

Author Hamlin Garland deftly captured the growing-up years of a young woman in nineteenth-century rural Wisconsin in his critically acclaimed *Rose of Dutcher's Coolly*. The novel was published in 1895.

> *Rose began to work early, but her work, like her playing was not that of other girls. As she never played with dolls, caring more for her hobbyhorses, so she early learned to do work in the barn. From taking care of make-believe stick horses, she came easily to take care of real horses.*
>
> *When a toddling babe, she had moved about under the huge plow-horses in their stalls, and put straw about them, and patted their columnar limbs were her little pads of palms, talking to them in soft indefinite gurgle of love and command.*
>
> *She knew how much hay and oats they needed, and she learned early to curry them, thought they resented her first trails with the comb. She cared less for the cows and pigs, but before she was ten she could milk the "easy" cows. She liked the chickens, and it part of her daily duty to feed the hens and gather the eggs.*

*She could use a fork in the barn as deftly as a boy by the time she was twelve, and in stacking times she handed bundles across the stack to her father. It was the variety of work, perhaps, which prevented her from acquiring that pathetic and lamentable stoop (or crook) in the shoulders and back which many country girls have in varying degree.*

*All things tended to make her powerful, lithe and erect. The naked facts of nature were hers to command. She touched undisguised and unrefined nature at all points. Her feet met not merely soil, but mud. Her hands smelled of the barn yard as well as of the flowers of the wild places of wood and meadow.*[13]

## STUDYING PLANT DISEASES

Dr. Harry L. Russell, professor of agricultural bacteriology in the College of Agriculture at the University of Wisconsin–Madison, became dean in 1907. Before that time, most attention to plant diseases was the purview of the departments of agronomy or of horticulture. Russell was born and grew up in Poynette, Wisconsin, attending the Madison university from 1884 to 1888 and then taking his graduate studies at Johns Hopkins University in Baltimore. He returned to Wisconsin in 1893 as assistant professor of bacteriology in the ag college.

Among his many outside duties, he advised in the establishment of the state's first pea canning plant in Manitowoc in about 1894. After studying black rot disease in cabbages growing in the Kenosha area, he published a major report in 1898, making it among the first such investigations in Wisconsin.[14]

## WISCONSIN AGRICULTURE ASSOCIATION FORMED

The Wisconsin State Agriculture Association was formed in March 1851 in Madison, based on a model developed in New York State. Since many Wisconsin farmers were from there originally,

Professor Lewis Ralph (L.R.) Jones almost single-handedly saved Wisconsin's cabbage industry when he developed a strain of the vegetable that was resistant to a particular blight. Jones was a professor of plant pathology in the University of Wisconsin–Madison's College of Agriculture and Life Sciences in the early 1900s. *Courtesy of the University of Wisconsin–Madison Archives, SO6534.*

it seemed a natural progression. The group raised initial funds by subscription and hosted a cattle fair in Janesville in October 1851. An early report lamented that "none of the western counties had any specimens on the grounds, and the northern counties but few." This group soon faded away, and by the 1890s, the organization of a "state fair" was taken over by the Wisconsin Department of Agriculture. In 1961, a seven-person exposition board took over the fair's direction.[15]

# WISE GUYS TALK COWS

The principal figures in the state's agriculture sphere have often been referred to as the "Seven Wise Men of Wisconsin Dairying." There were a mixed lot of scientists, farmers, breeders and scholars. The group included Chester Hazen of Ladoga; William Dempster Hoard of Fort Atkinson; Stephen Faville, Alpheus D. Faville and H.C. Drake of Lake Mills; W.S. Green of Milford; and H.C. Dousman of Waterford.

Hazen built one of the state's first commercial cheese factories, located in Fond du Lac County. Hoard published *Hoard's Dairyman*, launched in 1885, and went on to be Wisconsin governor from 1888 to 1890. He constantly urged his readers to improve their breeds. Stephen Faville was a noted dairyman who helped organize the Wisconsin Dairymen's Association and strongly supported the Farmers' Institutes of Wisconsin. His brother Alpheus was another well-known stock breeder, as was Green, longtime treasurer of the dairymen's organization. Dousman was president of the Wisconsin Dairymen's Association in 1878.[16]

# "FIGHTING" BOB LA FOLLETTE

Wisconsin senator Robert La Follette was noted for his liberal ideals and fighting spirit, battling for his state's farm families, among other progressive causes. La Follette served as a member of the United States House of Representatives (1885–91) and was the twentieth governor of Wisconsin (1901–6) and a United States senator (1906–25). He ran for president of the United States as the nominee of the Progressive Party in 1924, carrying Wisconsin and 17 percent of the national popular vote.

La Follette was born in a log cabin near the town of Primrose, near New Glarus. His grandfather was born in France and fought in the American Revolution. La Follette's father, Josiah, died when La Follette was only eight months old. Mary, his mother, married again when La Follette was six years old, to John Saxton, who was twenty-six years her senior. Saxton admired his stepson's potential and observed that the boy would "either turn out to be a very wonderful man or a very bad one." Toward the end of his stepfather's life and after his death, La Follette became the family's sole financial support, and at age eighteen, he ran the family farm.

In 1882, La Follette married the feminine firebrand Belle Case, a crusader for women's suffrage who spoke at county fairs and other local gatherings throughout Wisconsin. She had no problem debating and lecturing from the back of a farm wagon. Case was the first woman to graduate from the University of Wisconsin Law School. When she and La Follette married in 1882, they agreed to delete "to obey" from their wedding vows, a move that symbolized their commitment to individual independence.

Their sons were also active in politics. Robert Jr. served as a United States senator from 1925 to 1947, and Phil was the twenty-seventh and twenty-ninth governor of Wisconsin from 1931 to 1933 and 1935 to 1939. The brothers were among those instrumental in forming the national Farmer-Labor Party, which was a strong supporter of President Franklin D. Roosevelt and most of his New Deal policies during the Great Depression. During Phil La Follette's term in office, he pushed through the formation of the Wisconsin Agricultural Authority to help farmers and promote farm products and established a Department of Commerce to improve relations between government and business interests.[17]

## Pay Up

*William Horlick, Sr., founder of the Horlick Malted Mike Company, Racine, Wisconsin, will not receive any rebate from the town of Mount Pleasant on his income tax for 1912, amounting to $15,371.52, which he paid under protest last year, claiming that it was illegal and unlawfully assessed and exacted. The matter will probably be laid before the country board of review on income tax at its next meeting at Racine, and may ultimately be appealed to the courts of the state.[18]*

# WHO CAN BE A FARMER?

*"Any damn fool can be a farmer," Dad often said. But we knew plenty of damn fools who tried farming and went broke because they didn't budget time, money or resources, and didn't have the stamina or desire to work 14-hour days most of the year, but for successful farmers like Dad, farming was a calling, not just a way to earn a living.*

*Few things are more satisfying than seeing smooth black fields turn green as rows of new plants sprout in the spring, or seeing your barn filled with hay, your silo with corn, and your granary with golden oats at the end of the season. During the Great Depression, when money was scarce and jobs difficult to find, there was no better place to be than on a fertile farm. While people in the cities lost jobs and struggled to put food on the table, we always had work and an abundance of meat, vegetables and fruit, fresh in summer and canned in winter.*[19]

There is a lot of truth to the proverb of "cutting hay while the sun shines." The task was always a team effort, both in the old days and now. *Courtesy of the Chippewa Valley Historical Society.*

# Farmers Take Up Collective Struggle

The National Farmers' Organization (NFO) began in Iowa and moved into Wisconsin in the late 1950s, challenging escalating price increases on farm products through collective bargaining, much like traditional labor unions. In the summer of 1962, Wisconsin NFO members joined in a holding action to raise prices for livestock and grain by keeping them off the market. Although the results were inconclusive, the NFO remained a potent voice for the state's farmers. With expertise in milk, wheat, corn, soybeans, hog and cattle sales, the group developed extensive business relations with international commodity buyers. Annually, the organization negotiates better prices and sales terms for its farmer-members. The group eventually simplified its name to National Farmers.

Paul Olson, a dairy farmer from Taylor, Wisconsin, was elected to his fourth term as National Farmers' president in 2012. During the height of a controversy over Wisconsin Republican governor Scott Walker's successful efforts to end collective bargaining for public employees in 2011, Olson spoke out, saying:

> We support the right of everyone to bargain collectively. It is unfortunate that this basic negotiating tenet used in professional sports, aviation, agriculture and manufacturing, as well as many other segments of the American economy, is under severe pressure in Wisconsin and several other states.
>
> The issue isn't really about budgetary considerations, but more about limiting collective bargaining. Wisconsin's public employees have already offered to help the state's budget by agreeing to the financial and benefit concessions called for in the Wisconsin budget bill.
>
> National Farmers Organization is committed to the collective bargaining concept authorized by the Capper-Volstead Act that provides farmers the right to bargain as a group. And we uphold the men and women who provide basic services that protects and supports communities in rural areas and cities alike.[20]

Olson is a third-generation dairy producer who joined the NFO in 1969 and operates a five-hundred-acre diversified organic farm. He and his wife, Judy, own a 100-head Holstein dairy herd, with a total cattle herd of about 250.

## DEATH OF HENRY C. WALLACE, SECRETARY OF AGRICULTURE

Iowan Henry Cantwell (Harry) Wallace was a farmer, a journalist and a political activist, serving as the secretary of agriculture from 1921 until his death in 1924. He was the father of Henry A. Wallace, who also became a secretary of agriculture under President Franklin D. Roosevelt. The elder Wallace was also editor of *Wallaces' Farmer* from 1916 to 1921.

Wisconsin's agriculture community of the day was saddened to learn of the death of this patron of farming, who was a firm friend of the University of Wisconsin's College of Agriculture and Life Sciences. Wallace's death was noted in a university bulletin:

> *Word was received early this week of the death of Henry C. Wallace, Secretary of Agriculture. Mr. Wallace served in this capacity under Presidents Harding and Coolidge, and the agricultural interests of the country are losing a true friend and enthusiastic worker.*
>
> *At a visit to this College three years ago, Mr. Wallace told how he visited Wisconsin in the days when he first contemplated taking an agricultural course. He had given up the idea when he got an audience with former Dean Henry, who persuaded to make the agricultural field his life work and assured him that if he applied himself, a real future lay before him. In a way, the splendid work of Mr. Wallace is a tribute to the judgment and spiritual leadership of our former Dean.[21]*

A happy Wisconsin dairy goat gives a big smile for the camera. *Courtesy of the author.*

# THE YEAR IN AGRICULTURE

West Virginian Howard Mason Gore served briefly as the United States secretary of agriculture at the conclusion of the first presidential administration of Calvin Coolidge. Gore was in office until March 4, 1925, following the death of his predecessor, Henry C. Wallace, ten days before the presidential election in 1924. Prefacing the department's annual report, Gore wrote to Coolidge on November 17, 1924. The report provided a breakdown on crops, land use and animals for the preceding year, including detailed information on the individual states, including Wisconsin. That letter follows:

> *To the President:*
>
> *It becomes my solemn duty, Mr. President, to transmit the annual report prepared under the direction of the late Secretary of Agriculture, Henry C. Wallace. Although Secretary Wallace did not have an opportunity to consider the report in its final form, it has been carefully reviewed by representatives of the department who have been in close touch with him and who worked with him in its preparation, and is believed to represent his views regarding the state of agriculture and the work of the department during the period it covers. It is regrettable that the lamentable death of Secretary Wallace leaves his annual report in the present status. The method pursed in submitting this report appears to be the only practical one to meet the situation that presents itself.*
>
> *Respectfully, Howard M. Gore, Acting Secretary of Agriculture*[22]

# SWISS CHATTER

In a 1923 newsletter, University of Wisconsin agricultural experts discussed the ethnicities of the state's farm population and made the following wry comment:

Bryan and Beth Voegeli own 140 head of Brown Swiss dairy cattle, which are milked twice daily at their farm near Monticello, Wisconsin. The sprawling complex of barns, sheds, lofts and outbuildings lies between New Glarus and Monroe. The Voegelis' milk is then sold to the nearby Chalet Cheese Company. Voegeli is a fifth-generation dairy farmer who puts in up to fourteen hours a day, seven days a week, working around the 800-acre family farmstead. He also leases another 1,100 acres to grow corn, soybeans and wheat. Voegeli, of Swiss heritage, prefers raising the Brown Swiss cow, which he feels "has the best set of feet and legs and is more rugged than Holsteins." The high protein count in the Brown Swiss milk also makes it good for cheese. *Courtesy of the author.*

*Wisconsin makes more than 70 percent of the Swiss type of cheese made in America. Hundreds of native Swiss makers are engaged in Wisconsin factories. Inability to speak the English language fluently on the part of many of these men has always been a handicap in reaching this group along instructional lines.*[23]

## CHEESE AND BEER PAIRINGS

The first brewery in Wisconsin was opened in 1835 in Mineral Point by brewer John Phillips. A year later, he opened a second brewery in Elk Grove. In 1840, the first brewery in Milwaukee was opened by Welsh immigrants Richard G. Owens, William Pawlett and John Davis. By 1860, nearly two hundred breweries were operating in Wisconsin, more than forty of them in Milwaukee.

Wisconsin cheesemaking got off to a rollicking start with Mrs. Anne Pickett, who established the state's first commercial cheese factory in 1841. She worked from her farm kitchen in Fond du Lac County, using milk collected from neighbors' cows. Seventeen years later, in 1858, John J. Smith obtained Wisconsin's first cheese vat and made cheese for sale out of his Sheboygan County home. He even reached beyond the state to peddle his products. His brother, Hiram Smith, a farmer on the University of Wisconsin Board of Regents, then established the state's first full-scale cheese factory in 1859. He purchased milk from other dairy farmers or processed their milk in exchange for a percentage of the finished cheese.

In 1864, Chester Hazen built a factory in Ladoga in Fond du Lac County. His doubters laughingly called it "Hazen's Folly," but the critics were silenced when, after just one year of operation, the factory used milk from more than three hundred cows to produce his cheese. This success heralded the rapid growth of the cheese industry in the state, with Hiram Smith helping the push. The first building in Sheboygan County erected especially for operation as a cheese factory was constructed in 1867 by L.P. Fischer and M. McKinnon, two and a half miles west of Sheboygan Falls. After two years of successful operation, the factory was sold to Smith, who brought it under his growing business umbrella.

It wasn't long before the participants in the state's dairy industry realized the value in banding together to promote their cause. In 1893, the Wisconsin Cheesemakers' Association was formed. The Southern Wisconsin Cheesemakers' and Dairymen's Association, intended to further the aims and purposes of the makers of

While beer and cheese go together like a horse and carriage, high-end champagne and award-winning Wisconsin cheese go even better. *Courtesy of the author.*

Swiss, Brick and Limburger cheese, was organized in 1901. The Central Wisconsin Cheesemakers,' Buttermakers' and Dairymen's Advancement Association came into existence in 1913, and many smaller local organizations followed.[24]

# HISPANICS AND THEIR WISCONSIN CHEESE

A Hispanic presence in Wisconsin dates from the eighteenth century, when Spanish from Louisiana carefully monitored trade between St. Louis and the fur trading center of Prairie du Chien and patrolled the Mississippi River. By the 1720s, the area's Native Americans were already securing Spanish guns and clothing. The Spanish also supported the rebellious American colonials during the American Revolution.

The state's more contemporary Spanish-speaking links began in about 1910, when Mexican refugees settled here after the revolution in their own homeland. While there were only about one thousand individuals of Hispanic descent permanently living in the state in 1950, thousands more were migrant workers. As the need for farm laborers grew during World War II, additional Hispanics flocked to Wisconsin, primarily from Mexico.

Many stayed after the war and became citizens. They were eventually joined by thousands of Puerto Ricans and natives of other Latin countries. By 1970, more than 40,000 Hispanic residents considered Wisconsin their home. By the mid-2000s, some 194,000 Hispanic Americans lived in the state.

They naturally brought their cuisine, and their cheeses, with them. Today, Hispanic varieties have moved beyond the ethnic kitchen and restaurants to become favorites of the wider community. Food fans love working with Hispanic cheese because of the wide range of serving and cooking possibilities. There are three primary styles: fresh cheese, melting cheese and hard cheese.

Fresh cheeses are mild and crumbly in texture. What sets them apart from other Hispanic cheeses is that they do not melt when heated. While warm and soft, they do not lose their shape. This is an important factor in many dishes, such as enchiladas and chile rellenos, where the cheese is used as a stuffing and needs to maintain its form without getting soupy. White in color, fresh varieties include Queso Blanco, Panela and Queso Fresco. Originally, they were made by local cheesemakers and had a shelf life of less than one week. Today, they still taste fresh for up to three or four months. These cheeses are often eaten as a snack with fruit. They are also often crumbled on a salad or used as a recipe's base ingredient.

Melting cheeses, such as Queso Quesadilla, Asadero and Oaxaca, melt without separating into solids and oil. They are generally mild-tasting and make marvelous snacks. A must in quesadillas and tacos, melting cheeses are also great on pizza, in grilled cheese, on burgers and on tortillas and taco chips because they are less greasy and have more of a cheesy taste.

Hispanic hard cheeses have a strong flavor and a dry, crumbly texture and are used for grating. Cotija and Anejo Enchilada fall into this category. Traditionally, they were aged for up to a year outdoors.[25]

## LEMKE SEED COMPANY ESTABLISHED

Lemke Seed Farms was established in 1937 by Louis Lemke after attending a farm short course program at the University of Wisconsin–Madison and learning about the new discovery of hybrid seed corn. He returned home and planted half an acre that first summer, harvesting seven bushels of seed that he sold to neighbors. Throughout the 1940s and 1950s, Lemke raised and sold his Wisconsin certified hybrid seed corn and seed oats. His son, Ralph, joined the family business in 1960.

In 1967, single cross seed was introduced, and soybean seed was added in the 1990s. Grandson Rick joined the firm in 1997 after receiving a degree in agricultural business from Iowa State University and handles sales and marketing. His brother, Patrick, began with Lemke Seed after completing a similar farm short course that his grandfather had earlier attended in Madison. Patrick directs the warehousing, seed production and mechanical functions of the operation.[26]

# HOW ARE YOU GONNA KEEP 'EM DOWN ON THE FARM ONCE THEY'VE BEEN TO PAREE?

*George Engelhardt, who is engaged in general farming on a tract of land of one hundred and forty acres near Kansasville, was born in Paris township, Kenosha County, May 25, 1860, a son of John and Rachel (Beyer) Engelhardt, both of whom were natives of Germany. The father came to Wisconsin in 1853 and settled on a farm in Paris township, Kenosha County. He afterward purchased a farm in Dover township, Racine County, at twelve shillings per acre. It was a tract of wild land when it came into his possession, but with characteristic energy he transformed it into fertile fields, annually gathering good harvests.*

*He was married in Paris township and to him and his wife were born six children, all of whom are living: Kate, the wife of T.H. Hillman, a railroad man of Spooner, Wisconsin; Sophia, the wife of L. Hintz, a night watchman residing in Burlington; Carrie, the wife of Christ Olson, a railroad man of Spooner, Wisconsin; John, who is living in Brighton township; William, a farmer of North Dakota; and George.*

*The parents were members of the Lutheran church at Burlington and in his political views Mr. Engelhardt was a republican. He started out in business life empty handed and borrowed the money with which to pay his passage to the United States, but in this country he prospered, owing to his persistent, resolute purpose, and became the owner of a farm of one hundred and twenty acres of well improved and productive land.*

*George Engelhardt was educated in the district schools, after which he took up farming and has since carried on general agricultural pursuits save for about two years, which he devoted to railroading. He has an excellent tract of land of one hundred and forty acres, which he has brought to a high state of cultivation, annually gathering rich crops as a reward for the care and labor which he bestows upon the fields. He has twelve or fourteen cows which he milks and he raises cattle and hogs, having some high grade shorthorn cattle upon his place. His business affairs are carefully and wisely directed and success attends his efforts in substantial measure.*

*On the 13th of May, 1888, Mr. Engelhardt was married to Miss Tressie Rusburg, a native of Caledonia, Wisconsin, and a daughter of Charles Rusburg, a farmer, who became one of the early settlers of Caledonia township. The three children born of this marriage are: George, a farmer of Brighton township. Kenosha county; and Henry and Edna, both at home.*

*...He served for about twenty years as a member of the school board and the cause of public education has always found in him a stalwart champion. In fact, he stands for progress and improvement along many lines and does everything in his power to further the material, intellectual and moral development of the community.*[27]

## FARMING IN THE "CUT-OVER"

Approximately one-sixth of Wisconsin's farm families in the 1930s and 1940s lived north of a line extending from Brown to Marathon to Polk Counties. This area covered one-third of the state's land and one-fourth of its counties. It cost more per capita in relief, education, health, local government, roads and other public services than any other area of the state. Since the first federal relief appropriations were made in 1933, the region has continued to receive a disproportionally large share of state and federal relief expenditures. This area, the poorest in the state, had the highest annual birthrate and led in the number of unemployed young people migrating to cities in search of work. At one time, the region was heavily forested. By the early 1940s, however, it was largely cut over, with only a few islands of remaining virgin timber. Thus the region was called the "Cut-Over," a rough, raw land of rocks, stumps and marsh. The following is an excerpt from a 1941 study done on the inhabitants of that region:

*Although the Poles now rank second only to the Germans in the foreign-born and foreign-stock populations of Wisconsin, they are much more recent arrivals, as a group, than either the Germans or the third largest group, the Norwegians. Their migration to farms in Polandville followed the pattern which can be found in all other Polish farming localities of the "cut-over." With only a few exceptions, all heads of Polish families in our study are foreign-born, and Polandville is their second place of residence in America. Polandville was settled as the result of a landward movement from the Great Lake metropolitan-industrial region. The characteristic pattern includes a period of years in unskilled or semi-skilled urban labor in order to accumulate the necessary savings for land purchase.*

*This temporary industrial stop-over was not true of either of the other major European contributors to Wisconsin—Germans and Scandinavians—principally because of the relatively poorer financial condition of the Polish peasant immigrants. As savings were accumulated, they began to be drawn into the "cut-over" through the advertising media of land companies whose agents worked in the industrial centers. Land was cheap, they read, it was easy to clear, and it produced bumper crops of all varieties. Here was the opportunity to achieve the goal which induced them to migrate to America! Own a farm!*

*Unfortunately, not all land agents were as honest as they appeared to be. The "farms" too often turned out to be stony, stumpy undeveloped land that was suitable for cultivation only after an enormous cost in both money and labor. Beside the physical handicaps, there were others, and the story of one settler...is an example. He told of buying a piece of land, on one corner of which appeared to be a very desirable homesite that required a minimum of clearing. He recounted further how his neighbor encouraged him in his clearing efforts. Someone else in the neighborhood, however, suggested to the newcomer that he find out if he was really clearing his own land. This could be determined only with the aid of a survey. When this was made, the new settler found out that he had been on his neighbor's land, that most of his own forty consisted of swamp land.*[28]

# Raymond Township's Stellar Light

*Edward Brice is the owner of an excellent farm situated on section 7 of Raymond township and thereon he is successfully engaged in general agricultural pursuits and dairying. His birth occurred in Raymond township, December 2. 1858. His parents being Thomas and Alice (Drought) Brice. The mother was a native of Ireland but was only two weeks old when she was brought by her family to the new world. Her parents first settled in Canada, where they remained until she was twelve years of age.*

*Mrs. Brice then came to Racine County with her brother, making the journey in an ox cart. The entire district was wild and undeveloped and the Indians were still numerous in the neighborhood. There was much wild game to be had and the entire district was covered with its native growth of timber and grasses.*

*The brother built a log house and prepared the place for his parents who came the following year. Thomas Brice, the father of our subject, was born in Ireland and on coming to the new world spent a year at Coney Island, after which he removed to Racine County. He was about sixty-five years of age at the time of his death, his birth having occurred in 1824 while in 1889 he passed away. His wife, who was born in 1825, died in 1908, having reached the ripe old age of eighty-three years.*

*In their family were eleven children, of whom the following are yet living: Emily, the widow of Joseph Field and a resident of Manistee, Michigan; Jane, who married John Mathias and after his death was married to Wesley Ash but is again a widow and makes her home in Raymond Township; Eliza, the widow of William Killips, of Waukesha County; Amelia, Edward; Sherman, who married Eliza West and after her death married Matilda Christensen, his home being in Raymond township; and Frank. In his political views the father was a stalwart republican, always giving earnest support to the party.*

*He belonged to the Baptist church while his wife was a member of the Methodist Episcopal church. Both were early pioneers in this district although Mrs. Brice was here for some years before her husband's arrival, coming in 1838 almost before the seeds of civilization had been planted in the district. There was no phase of frontier life with which she was not familiar—the log cabin with its fireplace and tallow candles and the uncut forests. All these were features of the district when she arrived and her father, George Drought, who came the following year, bore an active part in promoting the pioneer development of the region.*

*Edward Brice obtained his education in the district schools and worked on the farm through the summer months, the winter seasons being devoted to the acquirement of his education. When his textbooks were put aside he gave his entire attention to farming and following his mother's death he and his sister and brother purchased the old home place on which he yet makes his home. The farm comprises one hundred and six acres of rich and productive land which he has brought to a high state of cultivation where his practical and progressive methods are manifest in the excellent crops which he annually raises.*

*He has put up new buildings and part of the modern equipment of his place is a large silo. In connection with general farming he does some dairying and both branches of his business are proving profitable. In fact in all matters relating to the farm he displays sound judgment and unaltered enterprise and his success is the result of his labors.*

*In politics he is a republican but is inclined to the independent forces and he has never sought nor desired office, preferring to concentrate his entire time and attention on his chosen occupation.*[29]

# STRIKE OUT

When agitation grew in Wisconsin for a wheat strike to improve prices, the Wisconsin Farm Bureau Executive Board declared on October 29, 1920:

*The Wisconsin Farm Bureau Federation does not endorse "strikes" as a means of controlling the price of farm products;*

*however, we do insist that if our farmers are to continue producing farm products they must receive a margin over the cost of production. Also we believe that every farmer has and should have the right to sell his products at such a time as market demands insure [sic] a reasonable price…*

*It would be good business policy for farmers to discontinue heavy marketing and allow the market to adjusted itself. Wisconsin farmers are willing to stand their share of losses incurred as a result of natural deflation uncommon with other classes, but not for unfair practices and manipulated inequalities.*[30]

## FANCY FOOTWORK EXPECTED

In the early 1920s, agricultural students at the University of Wisconsin were excited about the new barn being erected on campus and looked forward to celebrating, as evidenced in a school newsletter:

*Exterior construction of the new beef cattle barn is nearing completion (at the University of Wisconsin's College of Agriculture). The building is 108 by 40 feet and the first story provides room for about fifty breeding animals of the College beef herd, while the second floor has storage space for about fifty tons of roughage. Grain bins and a feed room are provided on the first floor and a silo of 150 tons capacity is at the north end of the building.*

*On Saturday night, November 1, the Agric and Home Ec students have arranged a barn dance in the new building. Members of the faculty are invited to join the student body on this occasion, which offers a splendid opportunity for an informal get-together of staff members and students.*[31]

# FARM ACTIVIST INVOLVED IN COMMUNITY

Farm activist George McKerrow of Pewaukee was elected president of the Wisconsin Farm Bureau in 1921. He received a salary of fifteen dollars per day for a maximum of two hundred days, plus expenses. The federation inventory that year listed assets of two desks, four chairs, one table, one mimeograph machine and one typewriter. Despite his hard work on behalf of the bureau, McKerrow needed to resign in April 1923 to manage his own farming operations.

McKerrow had a distinguished career in farming, including a stint on the Wisconsin State Board of Agriculture; positions as vice-president of the National Horse Breeders' Association, lecturer for the Wisconsin Farmers' Institute and president of the Wisconsin State Fair; and memberships in the Farmers' National Congress and the Wisconsin Good Roads League.

He was interested in purebred horses and brought the first Percheron horse from France to Waukesha County in 1872, the magnificent LeGrande Monarch III. McKerrow also imported sheep and raised Merino, Cotswold, Leicestershire, Oxford and Southdowns, being the first Waukesha County farmer to specialize in the raising of registered sheep. His sheep were shipped to other raisers throughout the United States and Canada.

McKerrow was known for his strength, as well as his membership in the Prohibition Party. The town of Lisbon held its annual town meeting in 1886, and the thirty-four-year-old McKerrow was there, along with a neighbor, Jack Edwards.

A newspaper clipping from the April 1886 *Waukesha Democrat* described

> *a new and manly way of making political converts. It is said of Jack Edwards, a prominent Republican of the Town of Lisbon, just previous to the Town of Lisbon meeting met on the road, George McKerrow, who is a leading prohibitionist of that town and thereupon a lively political discussion was had. They finally agreed to wrestle...the one losing to be of the politics of the winner. At it they went, and both being*

*strong, able-bodied men, the contest was a warm one, and twice did Jack go to grass. Now there is a Prohibition Jack in Lisbon.*[32]

McKerrow was ninety-three when he died in 1946.

## HELPING GARDENS GROW

J.W. Jung, with the help of his brother, Louis, launched a seed company from their parents' farmhouse in 1907. J.W. and his wife, Minni, went on to expand the business into one of the nation's premier garden and catalogue companies. Company president Richard Zondag wrote the following as an introduction to a centennial booklet produced by the company:

*One hundred years ago, my grandfather planted a seed that continues to bear fruit. That "seed" was the founding of the J.W. Jung Seed Company in 1907—a venture he set off on at a young age, full of determination and full of wisdom.*

*His upbringing on the family farm taught him much about plants but Grandpa never stopped learning. He relished opportunities to learn more about plants and how to do things better. Above all, he understands the grace of God that he and his family were blessed with.*

*Today we are celebrating his legacy. The company he launched in his parents' home in rural Wisconsin has become a national player in the home gardening industry, providing seeds, stock and supplies to gardeners throughout the United States. And, like Grandpa, we relish opportunities to learn, always with the customer in mind.*

*We have been blessed with many friends and supporters over the years. All of you have been instrumental in helping nurture this business, and I am sure that Grandpa is looking down on us with approval. His goal remains ours: to provide the best seeds and stock for northern climates, at reasonable prices and with excellent service.*

*As we celebrate one hundred years in business, we recommit to J.W.'s principles while sharing the wonder, awe and satisfaction he knew could only come from home gardening.*

By 2012, J.W. Jung Seed company had five retail garden centers and a variety of catalogues describing everything from delicate roses to tantalizing tomatoes, developed at an 180,000-square-foot facility that does enough business to require its own ZIP code. The company divided its operations in 1997, with the Zondag family keeping J.W. Jung Seed Company, and the Jung family operating the farm seed business, Jung Seed Genetics. In 1988, the Zondag operation acquired McClure and Zimmerman's bulb catalogue and now ships 8 to 10 million catalogues per year.[33]

# FARMING IS THE BERRIES

*In the spring of 1857, we commenced gardening for market, though it was in a very small way. There were then no reliable lines to any outside market. The home market was a poor and uncertain one. Altogether the prospect was by no means an encouraging one. Yet we concluded to try it and do our best.*

*We sent out oldest son, then a bright little fellow, over to town with (strawberries). He was told that he must get 12½ cents per quart for them. They were nicely hulled and put up in full potato measure.*

*Our boy returned without selling a single berry, saying that one lady offered him 10 cents for one quart, but as he was told he must get 12½ cents, he did not accept it, but brought them all home. This was surely not very encouraging.*

*The following summer, I traded my first bushel of berries to a merchant for a barrel of flour.*[34]

The farm market on Madison's Capitol Square always brings out a crowd. *Courtesy of the author.*

## ALICE IN DAIRYLAND

From pastoral beginnings following World War II to today's instant media, Wisconsin's Alice in Dairyland promotion has changed with the times. But Alice remains a one-year contractual position with the Wisconsin Department of Agriculture, Trade and Consumer Protection (WDATCP) as Wisconsin's "Agricultural Ambassador."

In 1948, the first Alice was Margaret McGuire of Highland, a young woman fresh out of high school who competed in a field of five hundred entries. She earned a master's degree in elementary education and taught school for twenty-three years. Interestingly, Muscoda's Jill Makovec, the sixtieth Alice, lived only a few miles away from her earlier predecessor.

Four Alices in Dairyland (Merrie Barney, 1959; Beth Bartosh, 1964; Janice Findlay, 1976; and Laura Oldenberg, 1978) were from

Burlington in Racine County when they were selected. Ladysmith, Fort Atkinson, Green Bay and Oregon were each home to two Alices.

Over the years, the winner has evolved into a public relations professional with at least four years of experience or education in agriculture, public relations, communications or related fields. Once hired, Alice garners more than $1 million worth of free airtime and print space for Wisconsin's food, fiber and natural resources industry. She earns a salary of $40,000, plus travel and health expenses, along with gaining professional experience and contacts.

Among those who have gone on to business careers was Beverly Steffen Brunner, the 1952 Alice, who worked for General Mills in Minneapolis before moving to Los Angeles, where she became a food stylist for print and television media. Mary Ellen Jenks, the 1953 Alice, became a vice-president for the Green Giant and Pillsbury Companies.

Katie Wirkus served as the sixty-fourth Alice in 2011–12, logging thousands of miles over her term and making hundreds of appearances. Wirkus was actively involved on her family's dairy and swine farm in Athens, as well as in 4-H. She graduated from the University of Wisconsin–River Falls with degrees in agricultural education and mathematics.

Early Alices had a doll taller than themselves created in their likeness and showcased during the Wisconsin State Fair. Joan Engh (1960) went on to become Miss Wisconsin in 1962 and was a runner-up in the Miss America pageant.[35]

## "FEED THE SOIL!" SAYS 2008 MOSES FARMER OF THE YEAR

Nicholas, Gary and Rosie Zimmer of Otter Creek Organic Dairy in Avoca, Wisconsin, were named 2008 Organic Farmers of the Year by the Midwest Organic and Sustainable Education Service. In 2003, Linda Halley and Richard DeWilde of Harmony Valley Farm in Viroqua, Wisconsin, were also honored as MOSES farmers for that year.

Gary and Rosie Zimmers and their son, Nicholas, were named Farmers of the Year for 2008 by the Midwest Organic & Sustainable Education Service. They manage their 1,290-acre Otter Creek organic dairy farm in Avoca, Wisconsin. *Courtesy of the Midwest Organic & Sustainable Education Service.*

According to the organization, the Zimmers managed 1,200 acres of organic crops, including alfalfa, grass forages, corn, soybeans, canning peas, oats, barley and rye. They also milked two hundred cows and have fifty dry cows, three hundred heifers, one hundred beef cattle and one hundred pasture-raised feeder pigs.

The MOSES newsletter reported:

*This farm is an integrated system of agronomy and animal husbandry. Key elements include tightly managed crop rotations; use of diverse forage blends featuring various legume and grass varieties; and multiple weed control methods (rotary hoe, cultivator, flame cultivator, cover crops, and interseeded crops).*

*Soil fertility is addressed through composting techniques to recycle livestock manure; green manure crops used as plow downs; subsoiling; and the use of purchased nutrients (especially calcium, sulfur and trace elements) to maintain maximum fertility and nutritional value of crops. Soil and water resources are managed tightly as well, since erosion is a major risk on this farm with rolling hills. When their farm received over twenty inches of rain during August 2007, no erosion occurred!*

*Prevention is the key to managing health problems in their animals. Animals are housed in clean, comfortable free stall buildings. Calves are weaned late. Livestock are outside in fresh air and rotationally grazed. The Zimmers grow their own excellent quality feed, and utilize mineral supplementation.*

*The Zimmers' marketing strategies are also diversified, with local sales of cheese and meats direct to consumers at their nearby "Local Choice Farm Market" operated by Rosie. Peas are sold to two processors for freezing. Milk was previously shipped to Organic Valley but is now made into a variety of cheeses and sold at the Farm Market and other venues.*

*It can easily be said that everyone in the organic community has been helped by Gary Zimmer. He has been a long time educator of all farmers. He founded Midwestern Bio-Ag in 1984, providing soil consulting services across the Midwest. Gary has written numerous books including The Biological Farmer, and given hundreds of presentations, including internationally. Gary challenges the thinking of organic farmers to understand their soils and what it takes to build healthy soils on their farms. As Gary has said many times, "A biologically balanced healthy soil makes for healthy plants, animals and humans."[36]*

# ICE SKATING MADE FOR FARM FUN

In his memoir, David Uihlein Sr. looked back on his growing-up years spent at Afterglow, the family's farm north of Port Washington, Wisconsin. During the winter, his father, Joe, nicknamed "Opa," made a skating pond for area kids. However, this always worried young Uihlein's mother:

*Much to Oma's consternation, who had visions of catastrophe, Opa loved highballing the old truck out on the thick winter ice coating the pond near the chicken house. The pond spread over a low-lying site, now mostly overgrown with cattails and junk trees. Opa popped the clutch and spun like a merry-go-round on the glassy surface, with everyone hanging on tightly in the back. But the pond was more appropriately used for ice skating. The surface was cleared by a blade mounted in front of one of the tractors.*

Afterglow Farm manager Steve Sandin shows off one of his marvelous cabbages. Vegetables grown at Afterglow Farm, one of southeastern Wisconsin's largest Community Shared Agriculture (CSA) producers, served numerous clients for almost a decade in the early to mid-2000s. The project was started by Lynde Uihlein, granddaughter of Joe Uihlein, to elevate the role of food, agriculture and the environment through healthy, sustainable practices, plus provide creative educational opportunities for families. *Courtesy of the author.*

Since there were not playgrounds for rural kids in those days, many of the neighborhood's farm youngsters were welcome to visit for hockey or to show off their figure-skating skills. Among them were Milton and Jean Karrell's six kids, who lived a half-mile west of Afterglow and the Poulls from the adjacent farm. The latter children sometimes packed into the manure spreader, albeit load frozen, and tractored over to Afterglow's pond. The Bialziks—Patsy, Greg, Paul, John, Bob, Marilyn and Ruthie—were also regular visitors to the winter pond. The entire mob then thawed out in the basement of the farm caretaker's house, since no outside bonfires were allowed by Opa.

Afterwards, Opa brought out mugs of steaming hot chocolate to help warm the skating parties, much to their delight. Sometimes there would be simply big slabs of chocolate or peanut nut rolls to share. The sweets offset his reputation of being cantankerous, much of which was just bluster. Oma, on the other hand, was considered "a blessed lady" by the Poulls. She brought gifts to their farmhouse whenever a new child was born into that family.[37]

# There Is Always Plenty of Work on a Farm

Farmer Tom Heath told of a conversation with his dad in the 1940s:

My dad said if you're a farmer there is three things. He says, "You'll never go hungry. You'll never get rich. You'll never run out of a job."

And I said, "Why in the hell can't a farmer get rich as well as anybody else?"

He said, "If they did, who would do all the work?"[38]

# The Animals

*En gut schwein et all ("A good pig eats all").*
*—Wisconsin German farmer[1]*

## VALUE OF CALVES

William Dempster Hoard, founder of Hoard's Dairyman, always stressed the value of dairying and suggested that farmers "substitute the cow for the plow." A strong advocate of developing dairy breeds for milk production, he was a regular speaker at conferences around the country. He had this to say about calves:

> *From my earliest infancy down to today…I was brought up along with bovine babies. I have had a deep interest in the little animal called the calf, and, as a consequence, at an early age I made something of a study of the animal. Calves are very much alike, whether they come from one breed or another. As rule, those who had had experience in dealing with them discover that a thoroughbred calf is the most intelligent. There is a long line of heredity in its behalf but the most provoking thing on this green earth at times is a calf. He will stand and regard you with a look of mild and innocent baby-like wonder and a stupidity that is unfathomable.[2]*

# COWS GALORE

What better animal could there be to represent Wisconsin than the dairy cow? There are about twelve thousand dairy farms in the state, with more 1.26 million cows producing an average of 20,630 pounds of milk each per year. Black-and-white Holsteins are the most popular milk cows in Wisconsin, making up more than 90 percent of the state's herds. The Holstein's popularity stems from its ability to produce more milk than any other breed. Holsteins originated in northern Holland and Friesland. Holsteins are also becoming more popular due to the increase in demand for lean beef.

Cheesemakers use almost all of this milk to produce cheese at 129 plants today. In 1922, there were 2,800 cheese factories. In 1945, some 1,500 cheese factories produced about 515 million pounds of cheese per year.

Wisconsin has more skilled and licensed cheesemakers than any other state. These cheesemakers must complete rigorous studies in dairy science and cheesemaking before they can be licensed. They also may serve as apprentices under licensed cheesemakers. Additionally, Wisconsin is the only state to offer a master cheesemaker program, patterned on the rigorous standards of similar programs in Europe.

These craftsmen produce more than 2.6 billion pounds of cheese each year, which amounts to 25 percent of all domestic cheese.[3]

# LOTS AND LOTS AND LOTS OF LACTOSE

*How much is ten billion pounds of milk, Wisconsin's yearly output? Think of it! Think of it flowing over Niagara Falls, harnessed to machinery, turning the wheels of industry, lighting our homes, and moving the traffic on our streets! Yet this is exactly what it does. It is the life blood of our Commonwealth. It furnishes to the people of Wisconsin more than one quarter of their total income.*[4]

## ANCESTOR COWS

Wisconsin's first registered Holstein bull was Elswout Prince 95 HHB, purchased in 1873 by Septer Wintermute of Whitewater. The first registered female Holstein of record was Lillian 365 HHB, acquired in 1877 by Gran and Van Waters of West Salem. The first native Wisconsin-registered Holstein was Lottie Douglas 1034 HHB, born May 24, 1877, in the herd of T.W. Laramy in Beloit.[5]

## HOOFING IT

The famous racehorse Dan Patch threw a shoe while warming up at the Wisconsin State Fair in 1904 and was brought to a local blacksmith for a new shoe. The hoof fragment, now owned by a private collector, could be the only existing piece of the country's greatest horse racing champion. Never losing a race, Dan Patch earned the title of being the "World's Champion Harness Horse" and the "greatest harness horse in the history of the two-wheel sulky." His world record of 1.55 for the mile is a record unbroken. The horse traveled in its own private railcar.[6]

## ALL IT TAKES FOR CHEESE IS COWS

Stephen Faville was a noted dairyman from the Lake Mills area who came to Wisconsin from New York. He was often asked to lecture on the subject of milk, cheese and raising dairy cows. The following is from a talk he gave at the ninth annual meeting of the Wisconsin Cheesemakers' Association:

> *Myself and two brothers came to Wisconsin in 1844 and all we knew how to do was to make cheese, and in 1845 we made some and soon got into the factory system, because some of us had enough cows to make it pay without securing other milk. We hired*

Antoinette, a fiberglass Holstein cow, was erected in Plymouth, Wisconsin, as a symbol of the city's dairy heritage. The twenty-foot-high and thousand-pound bovine was set up in 1977 for Plymouth's centennial. It recalls the Wisconsin Cheese Exchange, located in the city in the late nineteenth century. *Courtesy of the author.*

*our neighbor's cows at first, and paid him so much cheese a month for the use of his cows. We had no fences to keep the cows inside of, but we had two cows that had young calves, and we tied up the calves and the mothers staid* [sic] *with them and the rest of the cows staid* [sic] *with the mothers.*

*In the fall of 1847, we decided to increase our dairy, and I went down to Waukesha and bought forty cows. They cost me $11.50 a head, and thirty if them had big calves that thrown in. Later on, all that stock fell into my hands and I concluded to make cheese alone. I exhibited a cheese weighing ninety pounds in the first state fair held in Wisconsin, I think, in 1849 at Janesville. In 1857, I sold out that dairy farm but cheese was made on the farm continuously until the commencement of the factory system.*[7]

# ROOTING AROUND

Early Wisconsin hogs were not the sleek, shapely looking creatures seen on farms today. The original "prairie racer" was tall, lean and bristly, with a neck almost as long as the rest of its body. The tusky snout made it look more like a wild boar. It was also troublesome, causing farmers to devise all sorts of hog-tight fences. But even stout nine- or ten-rail fences were not enough to contain these beasts. With their long necks, they could push through the second and third rails, reaching out to root up three rows of potatoes if planted too close to the pens. These hogs matured late, and their meat was considered "only tolerable."

They were usually brought into the state by drovers from southern Indiana and Illinois to be sold to Wisconsin farmers. These were generally swine allowed to run free in the woods, with no attention paid to breeding stock. Subsequently, they were admittedly a wild lot.

Champion hogs take a break at the Wisconsin State Fair. *Courtesy of Jim Brozek.*

By the late 1850s, Wisconsin swine raisers began importing such breeds as the Suffolk. S.B. Edwards of Troy, Wisconsin, became one of the leaders in improving varieties of hogs in the state. Eventually, Yorkshires, Chester Whites, Sheffields and Essexes appeared on farms.

These pigs were often called "mortgage-lifters" when farmers were faced with bankruptcy as the wheat markets collapsed in 1870s and they needed fast cash from pork sales to save their property.[8]

## Beef and Hogs Talk It Up

In a notice sent around to University of Wisconsin agricultural staff and students in 1923, everyone was urged to check out the state's best swine:

> The Third Beef and Swine Demonstration will be held at the Stock Pavilion on Saturday, April 28, at 9:30 a.m. Observation of the cattle and especially the results of recent feeding trials will precede a carcass demonstration. At 11:00 o'clock, two steers, one from each lot, will be slaughtered and the carcasses exhibited.
>
> Swine being fed experimentally to study the comparative value of several supplements to corn, such as skim milk, chopped alfalfa, middlings, and several combinations of these feeds, will be shown.
>
> Charles E. Snyder, editor of the Chicago Daily Drover's Journal, will speak on livestock marketing in the auditorium of Agricultural Hall at 7:30 Friday evening, April 27, and again at the Stock Pavilion at 10 o'clock on Saturday morning.[9]

## Being Sheepish in Wisconsin

Walworth County led the state in the production of fine wool sheep in the 1850s. Breeders around Whitewater won numerous awards at the state Agricultural Exposition each year. In 1850, Whitewater had 3,282 sheep, more than any other area in Wisconsin. In 1860, the number dropped to 2,734, which was still more than elsewhere. In 1870, the flocks rose again, to 6,030. Whitewater's nearest competitor that year was Sugar Creek, also in Walworth County, with 5,449, while Racine County's Mount Pleasant registered 5,432. An average of six pounds of wool could be sheared from these animals.[10]

# Tossing Your Chips

The Wisconsin State Cow Chip Throw and Festival is held every year the Friday and Saturday of Labor Day weekend in August at Marion Park, Prairie du Sac, Wisconsin. As of 2012, the cow chip throw state record was 248 feet. In addition to adult throws, events include those for corporate teams and kids.

In 1975, the Sauk Prairie Jaycees gave the entire Sauk Prairie Area recognition as the Cow Chip Capital of Wisconsin and organized the first State Cow Chip Throw. In 1989, the Wisconsin state legislature proclaimed the cow chip the unofficial state muffin.

The first memorable cow chip unit in the event was the papier-mâché chip built on a three-wheeler. Other units that have been created and used include the cow chip factory, which sent chips out of a barn on a "conveyor," and a cow patty, a life-size cow that could really fling 'em.

In 1989, members of the Wiscowchip Committee built eight three-dimensional cows and a bull that were placed on wheels for a drill team called Bovine in Motion. That year, Bovine accepted an invitation to perform during halftime of a University of Wisconsin Badgers football game with the UW Marching Band and also appeared with the UW Varsity Band in the field house.

In 1990, the tallest parade unit was Cowabunga, standing at thirteen feet, six inches, with a head that moves from side to side. When she lifted her tail, an infamous "chip" tumbled out.[11]

## IMPORTANCE OF GOOD BREEDING

*In order for a man to get his money back in raising stock, he must select well-bred mares that are good individuals, breed them to a stallion that is well-bred, that is a good individual and whose ancestors were good individuals, keep his brood mares in good condition when carrying their foals, give them plenty to eat to produce a good flow of milk while suckling them, then feed the young things with judicious liberality after they are weaned and keep them free from vermin and worms at all times.*[12]

## CHAMPION HORSEFLESH

Most of the champion horses exhibited at the Wisconsin Agricultural Society Exposition up to the Civil War were Morgans and Blackhawks. The latter were a strain developed from breeding so-called blood horse stock from the original Justin Morgan, progenitor of the Morgan line. A blood horse could be an English thoroughbred or an Arab. The lines descended from these animals were favored by Wisconsin's cavalry regiments during the war. Strong, wiry, fast and spirited, they were prized for their medium size.[13]

## COUNTING YOUR CHICKENS

*The farm chicken population has actually declined in Wisconsin in the nearly forty years covered by crop reporting service records. In 1924, there were 13,680,000 farm chickens; a peak was reached in 1944 with 19,211,000; in 1962, there were only 10,211,000. Broiler chicken production, however, grew from 350,0000 in 1934 to 17,390,000 in 1962, reflecting the trend toward mass production of poultry for market.*

*Improved breeding and feeding for laying hens and pullets kept egg production from declining in proportion to the drop in farm chicken population. Egg output reached an all time peak in the state in 1944, with 2.4 billion eggs, but has since been holding fairly steady just under 2 billion—in 1963, Wisconsin produced about 1.8 billion eggs, 3.1% of the national total, putting us 11th among the states in egg production.*

*The really spectacular growth in the poultry field has come in turkeys. Wisconsin had only 433,000 turkeys in 1941; 20 years later, the state count was 6,220,000, 6% of the United States total, and our rank was fourth in the nation in turkey raising. By 1964, the state had slipped to eighth rank with 3.9% of the nation's production.*[14]

## ROTARY CATTLE

*The Rotary Club of Superior is glad to announce the arrival of "Rotary Queen," a Holstein nine months of age and the product of thirty-four years of the best breeding. At present, she is the property of the Club and later, will be offered as a prize to some of the dairymen in the vicinity of Superior. Cattle already purchased*

A herd of Holsteins stands alert in a Monroe County field. *Courtesy of the author.*

*by the Club represent a cash value of approximately $10,000.
This dairy stock will be distributed to farms of approved credit
who have applied for the benefits of the rural credits plan put into
operation by the Club. This plan offers three services to the farm
who wants to secure stock in this manner: 1st, He has the services
of an expert buyer to secure the cattle; 2nd, There is a saving in
the buying and shipping cost from $20 to $25 per head; 3rd, He
has the advantage of getting his cattle on longtime payments. By
this plan, Superior Rotarians hope to cover the grass lands of
Northwest Wisconsin with valuable dairy herds.*[15]

# PHILIPP SAYS GOODBYE TO HOARD

Upon learning of the death of ex-governor W.D. Hoard at age
eighty-two, Governor Emanuel E. Philipp issued the following
statement:

*In the death of Governor Hoard, Wisconsin lost one of her truly
great citizens of his time, if we are to judge greatness by the
measure of genuine usefulness to the people.*

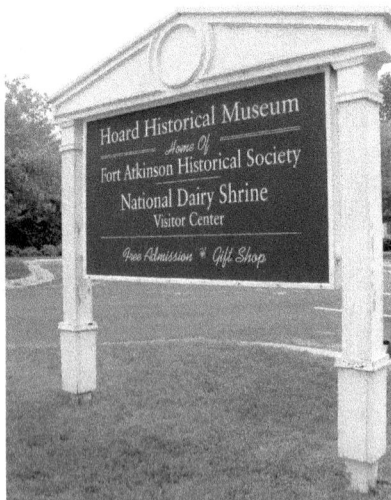

The Hoard Historical Museum
and the National Dairy Shrine
honor the memory of William
Dempster Hoard, founder of the
*Hoard's Dairyman* newspaper and
a longtime advocate of quality
breeding practices. The museum in
Fort Atkinson houses an extensive
collection of local memorabilia,
much of it focusing on Wisconsin's
dairy industry. *Courtesy of the author.*

*As a public servant he was a man of foresight and courage. In discussions, he was clear and convincing which made him a forceful advocate of those principles which he stood for. He rendered his greatest service to the public in the field of production. As a teacher in the better methods of farming, he was the recognized pioneer in scientific dairying and did more than any other man to promote that industry in Wisconsin.*

*His writings upon that subject have a general circulation throughout the northern states and his word was accepted as authority in the dairy sections of the country. He had a sympathetic nature, was public spirited, of pleasing personality, and had a sense of humor which made him a delightful company. Governor Hoard will long be remembered by the citizens of Wisconsin.*[16]

## GET IT RIGHT

Pioneer superstitions perhaps have elements of truth in them. Every farmer had his own suggestions on how to raise bumper crops.

For instance, in the coulee country along the Mississippi River near La Crosse, the locals agreed that meat butchered in the light of the moon would not shrink or fry away so much and would also keep well. Chicken also bleeds better and will can nicer, and the feathers will come off much easier.

Others said that carrots, turnips and other vegetables growing in the ground should be planted in the dark of the moon. Above-ground crops, such as corn, cabbage and lettuce, should be planted when the moon is light.

Be aware that a farmer who laughs too loud while planting corn is likely to get ears with uneven rows of kernels on them, and the kernels may be too far apart.[17]

# LOTS O' COWS

The Agricultural Extension Service of University of Wisconsin reported on the number of cows in Wisconsin in 1914:

> *Today, Wisconsin is the premier dairy state. She has a grand total of 3,000,000 dairy cattle which includes 80,000 purebred Holsteins, 20,000 purebred Guernseys, 8,000 purebred Jerseys. Wisconsin has more of each of one of these breeds that can be found in their original homes, in addition: 2,000 purebred Brown Swiss, 1,700, purebred Ayrshires. The state now has 90,000 silos, 3,000 cheese factories, 800 creameries, 70 condenseries and her annual dairy output is value at $300,000,000. Wisconsin is the home of the largest co-operative cheese marketing company in the United States, The Wisconsin Cheese Producers Federation, which will handle this year seven percent of the nation's entire cheese production….* [The state] *recently established a cheese grading system under which quality and price will be closely associated.*
>
> *Wisconsin dairymen are rapidly developing co-operative agencies for handling, storing and marketing dairy products. There is not a farmer, not a manufacturer, not a banker or any other businessman in the state of Wisconsin who does not owe a debt of gratitude to the dairy cow.*[18]

# TESTING PATENT AWARDED

In 1991, researchers at the University of Wisconsin–Madison were awarded a patent on a genetic test designed to help breed cows that produced more milk. The principal inventor was Charles M. Cowan, who developed the test for his doctoral thesis and who went on to serve as director of a genetics firm that was a subsidiary of the Tri-State Breeders Cooperative. Using Cowan's test, it was possible to identify animals that could produce 16,200 pounds of milk a year, 1,200 pounds more than average animals. Among others holding

*Above*: A fresh milk sign always signals a Wisconsin quality product. *Courtesy of the author.*

*Below*: An old tractor was still ready for use in a shed on a central Wisconsin farm. *Courtesy of Jim Brozek.*

the patent was Margaret R. Dentine, the first female faculty member in the Dairy Science Department at the University of Wisconsin–Madison. Lovingly nicknamed "Gretel," Dentine was also among the world's first researchers to apply molecular genetics to improve dairy cattle stock.[19]

## GETTING THEIR GOATS

The Wisconsin Dairy Goat Association was established in the 1930s and reactivated in 1946. There are now more than seventy-five families from Wisconsin and surrounding states who belong to WDGA. Wisconsin is the largest producer of fluid goat milk in the country and produces enough milk to support several specialty cheese manufacturing plants in the state, one fluid milk processor and two licensed farmstead cheese producers. Members' herds range in size from a few goats for home milk consumption to more than 300 in several commercial dairies. There are about 165 milking herds in the state including 19,506 milking does. Together, these animals produced 27.6 million pounds of goat milk in 2007.

The state's 180 milking herds produced 35.1 million pounds of milk in the last year. Milk sold at an average price of $30.25 per hundredweight (cwt.), with total receipts of $10.5 million.

Women are the primary operators of one-sixth of the dairy goat operations, one-third are men and about one-half are jointly operated. One-fourth of the primary operators are under age thirty-five, while only 3 percent are over age sixty-five. Most of the primary operators were involved in either a milk cow dairy or nonfarm occupation before beginning their goat milk operation.[20]

## MISTY MEADOWS FARM

Laura Doll Jay and her husband, Antony, raise two hundred milk goats on their Misty Meadows Farm north of Monroe, Wisconsin. Their days consist of 5:00 a.m. and 5:00 p.m. milkings of the

Nubians, LaManchas, Alpines and Saanens, that they have raised from babies (or "kids," in goat farmer language).

The young couple then sells the butterfat-rich milk to the Montchevre Betin dairy in Belmont, where it's processed into various cheeses for grocery stores and specialty shops. During the farmers' market season, the Jays peddle the cheese in Madison.

"I got my first goat, Misty, as a pet," says Laura. "We then named the farm Misty Meadows after her."

The couple began dairying in 2003, building milking stalls that handle eight animals at a time. "I started milking goats by hand, and that got pretty tiring," Laura recalls of their startup operations. "So we figured we needed a better system." The flock now produces about six hundred pounds of milk a day, and it's hard to keep up with the demand.

Antony's dad, Jeff—a design consultant for cheese factories in the United States, Mexico and Latin America—helped in the construction of their milking parlor. A native of Bath, England, the

A kid is a kid is a kid, unless it is a real kid. River Segel is pleased to make the acquaintance of a friendly farm goat. *Courtesy of the author.*

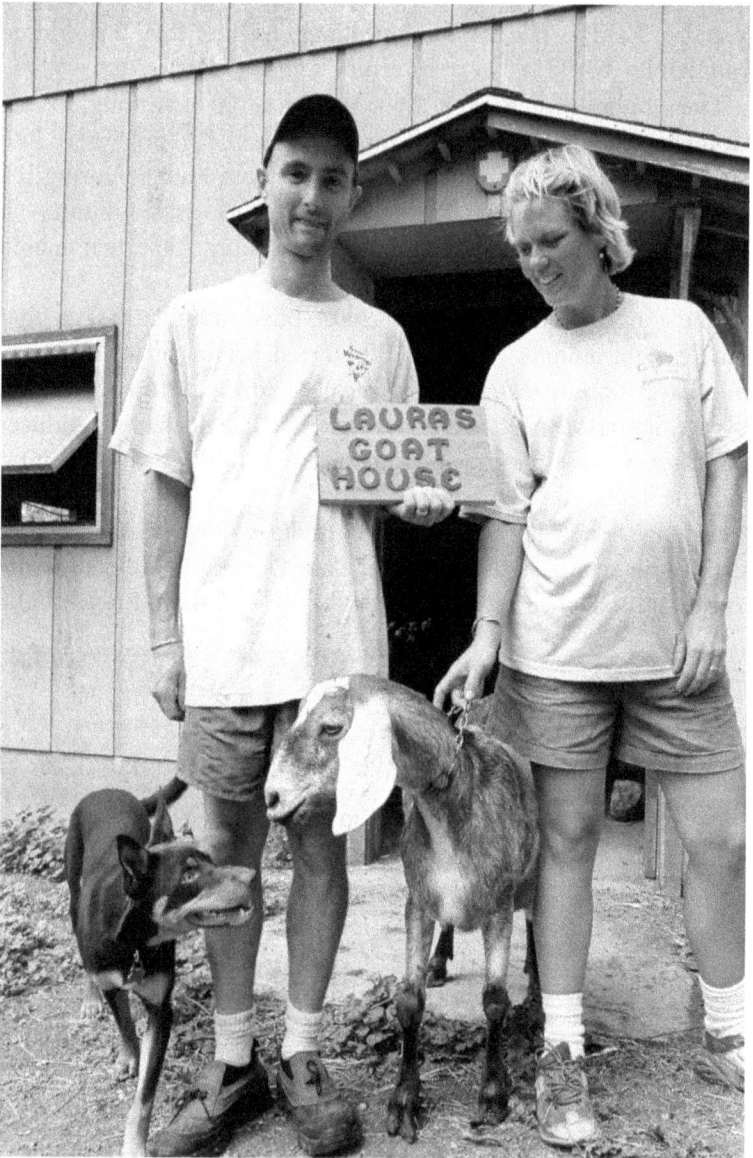

Antony and Laura Jay stand outside their "goat house" with Misty and a family dog. The couple raise goats on their farm near Monroe, selling milk to local dairies. In addition, they have also sold goats to farmers in Puerto Rico. *Courtesy of the author.*

elder Jay acted as immigration sponsor for his son, who met Laura seven years ago while the two worked at the Jung Garden Center in Madison. Laura is from Fox Point, a suburb of Milwaukee.[21]

## JUDGING SOWS

The *Wisconsin Agriculturist* offered good suggestions for hog breeders in 1900:

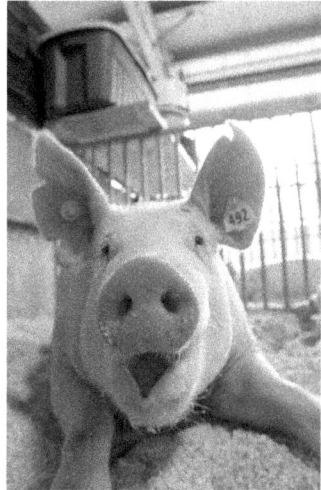

A porker at the Wisconsin State Fair says hello. *Courtesy of Jim Brozek.*

> *It is not always best to judge a young sow by her first litter. In most cases, if she is a good animal, each succeeding litter, for the first three or four at least, will be better than the last. No more serious mistake can be made by a farm than to allow a young sow to farrow one litter of pigs, fatten her for meat and then use the young sows for breeding. Keep well-matured sows as long as they farrow good pigs, discarding them only when they begin to fail.*[22]

# The Crops

*The proper time to plant corn is when the buds on the hickory trees are
as big as squirrel's ears.*
*—Norwegian pioneer saying, West Salem, Wisconsin*[1]

## ABE SPEAKS UP AGAIN

The following is an excerpt from a speech given by Abraham Lincoln
in 1859 to the Wisconsin State Agricultural Society in Milwaukee.
A plaque memorializing his address is on the Marquette University
campus, site of early Wisconsin state fairs before moving to West
Allis, Wisconsin, a Milwaukee suburb.

> *Again, a great amount of locomotion is spared by thorough
> cultivation. Take fifty bushels of wheat ready for harvest, standing
> upon a single acre, and it can be harvested in any of the known
> ways with less than half the labor which would be required if it
> were spread over five acres. This would be true if cut by the old
> hand-sickle; true, to a greater extent, if by the scythe and cradle;
> and to still greater extent, if by the machines now in use.*

Husking corn in 1910 on the Hanson farm in Racine County took plenty of hand labor, even augmented by "newfangled" machinery. *Courtesy of the Waterford Public Library.*

*These machines are chiefly valuable as a means of substituting animal-power for the power of men in this branch of farm-work. In the highest degree of perfection yet reached in applying the horsepower to harvesting, full nine-tenths of the power is expended by the animal in carrying himself and dragging the machine over the field, leaving certainly not more than one-tenth to be applied directly to the only end of the whole operation—the gathering in of the grain, and clipping of the straw. When grain is very thin on the ground, it is always more or less intermingled with weeds, chess, and the like, and a large part of the power is expended in cutting these.*

*It is plain that when the crop is very thick upon the ground, a larger portion of the power is directly applied to gathering in and cutting it: and the smaller to that which is totally useless as an end. And what I have said harvesting is true in a greater or less degree of mowing, plowing, gathering in of crops generally, and indeed of almost all farm work.*[2]

# WAR CAUSES CHANGE

The Civil War dramatically forced the spread of labor-saving farm equipment, even among those farmers who were suspicious of newfangled machines. The *Wisconsin State Journal* urged farmers to buy reapers since farm laborers, "the very bone and sinew of the harvest fields, will be called away to other fields of toil and danger." Every good reaper, the newspaper said, equaled five to ten men in the field. The Wisconsin State Agricultural Association reported that three thousand reapers were sold in 1860.[3]

# HOPS ON BOARD

Hops were grown in the American colonies almost as soon as first Europeans arrived. In the 1700s, New England was a major hops-producing region, since these émigrés sought raw materials with which to produce beer. Commercially produced hops were first introduced to Waukesha County in about 1837 by farmhands from New York who brought root stock with them. In 1842, the first hop farms appeared in Sauk County, which would become the heart of the hops industry with Kilbourn City (now Wisconsin Dells) as the processing hub. From 1860 to 1870, "the Wisconsin Hop Craze" created a lucrative business, particularly in Sauk County, Wisconsin, for returning Civil War veterans. The crop sold for fifty and sixty cents per pound. In 1860, Wisconsin produced 135,000 pounds of hops. By 1867, the state's production was over 6 million pounds. But the market had collapsed by the end of the 1870s when other growing areas of the country created a surplus.[4]

# BUMPER WHEAT CROP

By 1855, the Wisconsin wheat crop reached an impressive 9 million bushels. The next year, it was 12 million; in 1857, the figure hit 14 million. One speaker at the Rock County Agricultural Society and Mechanical Institute on September 27, 1855, was enthusiastic:

*Farmers are enjoying the good times…Fortune and plenty is vouchsafed to them all; stacks of grain crowning the ample fields of every farmer, granaries filled to overflowing; money plenty, old mortgages drawing from twelve percent up to fifty percent interest, canceled and discharge of record; surplus funds deposited with the gentlemanly bankers in our own county, in banks that never dream of failing; some change in the old wallet, old store debts paid up and receipted, and the cash system triumphant.*[5]

## NECESSITY MEANT INVENTIONS

*The problem for [pioneer] wheat farmers was in harvesting the crop. The basic tool, the scythe, was essentially unchanged since biblical times. The scythe was woefully inadequate for large fields of wheat, which needed to be harvested within days, and gathered by hand into sheaves for storage before threshing. The [farmer] needed either a large workforce, which meant wages, or better tools for harvesting. During the 1840s, Wisconsin inventors improved the threshers and harvester, laying the groundwork for Wisconsin's farm machine industry…*

*Jerome I. Case of Racine, who added a fan to help threshers separate grain from the outer chaff, built his own factory in 1847, producing a thresher with a two-tread [horse] power. Case's ten-horse sweep power thresher became the standard throughout the wheat-growing regions in the 1850s. The Wisconsin Farmer reported in 1850 that Case was building 100 threshing machines a year. By 1853, his market reached westward beyond the Mississippi. Case's company produce 300 threshing machine in 1860, 500 in 1865 and 1,500 in 1870…*

*Another Wisconsin inventor, George Esterly, produced what may have been the first successful American harvester in 1844. His Whitewater factory, built in 1857, produced reapers in*

In 1929, the Frost brothers, Dwight and Ray, tested an experimental model of the Rosenthal corn husker-shredder produced in West Allis, Wisconsin. Dwight stands by his McCormick 1530 tractor, while an unidentified man puts bundles onto the feed board. Ray is feeding the stalks into the shredder. The brothers later shared a corn husker-shredder between their farms and did custom shredding in the area. Corn pickers replaced the husker-shredders by the 1940s. The Frost farm was on Academy Road in the town of Rochester. *Courtesy of the Waterford Public Library.*

*Wisconsin until 1893 when Esterly decided Minneapolis was more centrally located to the railroads that served the wheat fields. Esterly is also credited with the invention of mowing machines and self-rake reapers, plus improved plows and seeders.*[6]

## GET BOGGED

Cranberries are common fruits indigenous to North America, native to bogs across the continent, with Wisconsin as the nation's leading commercial producer. Cranberries have been an important crop since the mid-nineteenth century, when the first commercial cranberry marshes were established in 1860 by Edward Sacket near Berlin, Wisconsin. They soon spread throughout central Wisconsin, with cranberry growers now annually harvesting enough cranberries to supply every man, woman and child in the world with twenty-six cranberries. Wisconsin not only produces the most fruit but also hosts the world's largest cranberry festival each fall in Warrens, Wisconsin. In 2004, Governor John Doyle declared the cranberry Wisconsin's official state fruit. October is National Cranberry Month.[7]

## UP IN SMOKE: A TIMELINE

1670: Father Jean Claude Allouez reports Indian nations growing tobacco on lands that would become Wisconsin.

1766: Jonathan Carver reports tobacco cultivation at Prairie du Chien.

1838: Future Madison mayor Elisha W. Keyes claims that his brother grows a personal crop of tobacco in Jefferson County.

1839: Wisconsin produces 115 pounds of tobacco.

1844: Ralph Pomeroy and J.J. Heistand plant the state's first designated tobacco crop.

1849: Wisconsin produces 1,268 pounds of tobacco.

1851: Tobacco is exhibited at the first meeting of the Agricultural Society and Mechanics Institute in Janesville.

1859: Wisconsin produces 87,340 pounds of tobacco.

1869: Wisconsin produces 960,813 pounds of tobacco.

1879: Wisconsin produces 10,608,423 pounds of tobacco.

Late 1800s–early 1900s: Dozens of tobacco warehouses are built in Edgerton during the crop's golden age, when the community emerged as the heart of the industry in Wisconsin.

1917: Swedish Match is founded.

1922: Growers centered in Viroqua in Vernon County organize the Northern Wisconsin Co-Operative Tobacco Pool. It folds in 1937.

1931: Wisconsin tobacco production covers 38,386 acres in twenty-two counties for a harvest of 76 million pounds; price plummets.

1933–38: Agricultural Adjustment Act sets federal standards for growing and selling tobacco—inaugurates price support system.

1938: Tobacco is cultivated on 8,310 acres in Dane County, out of 18,400 statewide.

1939: Wisconsin's tobacco crop is valued at $3,669,000 (roughly $56 million in 2009 dollars).

1941: Lancaster Leaf is founded.

1952: A paper published in the journal *Land Economics*, by the University of Wisconsin Press, reports that tobacco is the primary cash crop for 5,500 farmers in Wisconsin and that 7.5% of the total agricultural income in Dane County is from this source. The state haul is about $8 million (roughly $64 million in 2009 dollars).

1969: Philip Morris obtains a controlling interest in Miller Brewing, based in Milwaukee. It acquires the rest of the company the following year.

1972: Edgerton Tobacco Days launches.

1975: Madison adopts the nation's first ordinance regulating smoking, prohibiting it in most public places, including elevators, buses, theaters, museums and common areas of school buildings. This is expanded the following year to include more enclosed spaces.

1985: General Foods, which acquired Oscar Mayer of Madison in 1981, is acquired by Philip Morris.

1989: Philip Morris combines General Foods with Kraft.

1991: The UW–Madison adopts a smoke-free policy, prohibiting smoking inside buildings and vehicles. It is later expanded to include outdoor areas near entrances.

1992: The University of Wisconsin Center for Tobacco Research and Intervention is founded. It goes on to conduct extensive research and advocacy work in tobacco-use prevention, cessation and policy.

Madison adopts a plan to phase in a restaurant smoking ban. Restaurants are 100 percent smoke-free three years later.

USDA Census of Agriculture counts 1,722 Wisconsin farms growing tobacco.

1997: USDA Census of Agriculture counts 950 Wisconsin farms growing tobacco.

1998: A Tobacco Master Settlement Agreement is reached between the four largest United States cigarette manufacturers and attorneys general of forty-six states, including Wisconsin. Political controversy follows on how to allocate Wisconsin's share of the $206 billion settlement.

2002: USDA Census of Agriculture counts 452 Wisconsin farms growing tobacco.

2004: Tobacco Transition Program ends the quota and price-support system.

2005: Madison implements indoor smoking ban in bars and other enclosed public spaces but exempts cigar bars and private clubs.

2006: South Wisconsin farmers start test-planting burley tobacco, with investment from Philip Morris.

2007: Philip Morris spins off Kraft (including Oscar Mayer), which becomes a publicly traded company.

Wisconsin implements a smoking ban in colleges and hospitals.

Production contracts to produce organic crops are signed with Wisconsin tobacco farmers, led by the Organic Leaf Cooperative of Viroqua.

Edgerton's Tobacco Heritage Days festival is renamed Edgerton Heritage Days; the name is restored one year later.

USDA Census of Agriculture, the most recent to date, shows that seventy-two farms in Wisconsin cultivate tobacco; fifty-two of them are in Dane County.

2007–2009: The state's per-pack cigarette tax rises from $0.77 to $2.52.

2010: Wisconsin implements a statewide indoor smoking ban, including restaurants and bars.[8]

# Smoke 'Em If You Got 'Em

Walworth County appears to have been the site where tobacco was first grown by some enterprising settlers in 1844, though some authorities credit Fulton Township, Rock County, in the late 1840s. Whichever is the actual site, the initial effort was not a commercial success. The practical start of Wisconsin's fruitful tobacco industry came in 1853. Two farmers from Ohio, Ralph Pomeroy and J.J. Heistand, new in Wisconsin, sowed two acres of broadleaf near Edgerton in Rock County. When their crop was ready for market, they tied the leaves in conventional "hands," baled the lot and sold it locally for forty-two cents per pound.

The buyer, being short of ready money, bought on credit the first sound, commercial tobacco produced in Wisconsin. His intentions were good, but he fell by the wayside, and the sellers had to settle for fifty cents on the dollar. Not discouraged, the two farmers produced a larger and better crop and sold it for cash.

The two original farmers in Rock County had experimentally planted cigar-leaf tobacco using seeds then readily available in Ohio. The high quality of their crops suggested to other farmers that the soil of Wisconsin was especially suitable for cigar-leaf tobacco. Various importations of seeds into the state began to take place.

A Janesville farmer acquired Connecticut-Havana seed from Massachusetts in 1872. The resulting variety, known as Comstock Spanish, was soon being widely produced in the Wisconsin area where it was first grown. There were other importations of seeds of types growing around Lancaster, Pennsylvania, and in Connecticut. The older Wisconsin seedleaf tobacco developed from the latter was long locally called "Housatonic" or "big-seed" to differentiate it from Havana varieties.[9]

# Wisconsin Tobacco

Tobacco factories, centered in Milwaukee, were providing large-scale employment by the third quarter of the nineteenth century.

The census report of 1880 showed that 152 factories produced cigars valued at $1,346,925. The output of chewing and smoking tobacco and snuff, by three factories in Milwaukee, was valued at $978,281.

Cigars were much in demand, chiefly by Wisconsin's German population, and good rollers were much sought after. Prizes for extra output were frequently offered. One roller, William George Bruce, a Native American, related in his memoir that, while still in his teens in the 1870s, he had won a first prize: "$2.00 and free beer, having rolled up something over 5,000 cigars from Monday morning to Saturday noon." A good craftsman, his wages were eighteen dollars weekly.

The Internal Revenue Bureau of the time collected on all tobacco manufacturing and associated operations. The reported total of receipts from Wisconsin manufacturers, dealers, leaf handlers and others for the year 1880 came to $941,764.[10]

# VICTORY GARDENS

The Winnebago County agricultural agent offered a look a wartime gardens in his 1944 annual report:

> Sound gardening and fruit production practices have been promoted through the Victory Garden Program. This office has handled the allotment of city lots to city gardeners, has met with garden groups to discuss production and storage practices as well as disease and parasite control. Garden plans have been made and distributed.
>
> Monthly meetings, with a definite planned program are held by the Fruit and Garden Growers Association which is open to anyone interested. Garden and orchard tours, pruning demonstrations, exhibits of products have all been employed along with news notes, radio items and circular materials.
>
> Insect traps have been operated by interested cooperators. A spraying cooperative with twenty-six members and two spray outfits has been kept functioning.

*Meetings on butchering, cutting, storing, freezing and canning
have been held. This has been an important part of the program
of our Home Agent.*[11]

# THE BIG WIND

A thunderstorm with winds and baseball-sized hail struck the
countryside between Christie and Neillsville in late June 1934. The
hail fell on a mile-wide path moving in a northeasterly direction.
Farms with damage to homes, building and crops were those of
William Bahnsack, John Ripke, Hal Richardson, William Jurlburt,
Leo Kronberger, Alvin Jacob and Paul Jacob.[12]

# BIG-TIME GRAIN DEALER

Patrick P. Donahue, president of the Donahue-Stratton Company,
grain dealers of Milwaukee, was born in Walworth County on
May 27, 1863. His father, Thomas Donahue, a native of Ireland,
immigrated to Milwaukee with his wife, Mary Manion, and became
a farmer near Troy, Wisconsin.

After carrying on business independently, young Donahue formed
a partnership with H.M. Stratton, and

> *their interests were incorporated under the name of the Donahue-
> Stratton Company, with Mr. Donahue as president from
> the beginning and Mr. Stratton as vice-president. They do
> a cash grain business and operate the two largest elevators in
> Milwaukee. In 1909 they leased the Chicago, Milwaukee & St.
> Paul Railway elevator A, of one million bushels capacity, and
> operated it successfully until it was destroyed by fire in January,
> 1921. They then leased the Rialto on the Chicago & North
> Western Railroad with a capacity of one million six hundred
> thousand bushels and the Kinnickinnic elevator with a capacity
> of one million four hundred thousand bushels.*

*Mr. Donahue is the president of the Cooperative Orchard Company, which has a six hundred acre orchard at Sturgeon Bay. Of that tract of land five hundred acres is planted to sour cherries, being the largest sour cherry orchard in the United States. The balance of the land is planted to apples, plums and other fruits. Mr. Donahue is likewise interested in the Palmyra Enterprise, a weekly paper, which was established by his father-in-law, Oliver P. Dow, as a Prohibition paper.*

*He is likewise connected with a sheep feeding company at Manitowoc, feeding from five to ten thousand sheep at a time and also two hundred cattle. Mr. Donahue is the president of the feeding company and is thus controlling another large and important business enterprise. He is a man of marked capacity and power in business affairs, his labors constituting a dynamic force in bringing about progress in the business life of Milwaukee and the state. He readily recognizes and utilizes opportunities, and as the years have passed he has achieved success that is most gratifying.*

*Mr. Donahue has never been active in politics but maintains the position of a liberal democrat. His religious faith is that of the Catholic church. He loves all outdoor sports and greatly enjoys hunting, and he belongs to the Milwaukee Athletic Club, the Milwaukee Club, the Blue Mound Country Club, the Ozaukee Country Club and the Lake Shore Gun Club. He is also a member of the Rotary Club and his interest in the welfare and progress of the city is manifest in his connection with the Association of Commerce.*[13]

# THE STRAW PILE

In his book *Son of the Middle Border*, Wisconsin author Hamlin Garland ably captured what farm life was like. He describes the threshing days of his youth:

*We wished every day was threshing day. The wind blew cold, the clouds went flying across the bright blue sky, and the straw glistened in the sun. With jarring snarl the circling zone of dogs dipped into the greasy wheels, and the single-trees and pulley-chains chirped clear and sweet as crickets. The dust flew, the whip cracked, and the men working swiftly to get the sheaves to the feeder or to take the straw away from the tail-end of the machine were like warriors, urged to desperate action by battle cries. The stackers wallowing to their waists in the fluffy straw-pile seemed gnomes acting for our amusement.*

*The straw-pile! What delight we had in that! What joy it was to go up to the top where the men were stationed, one behind the other, and to have them toss huge forkfuls of the light fragrant stalks upon us, laughing to see us emerge from our gold cover. We were especially impressed with the bravery of Ed Green who stood in the midst of the thick dust and flying chaff close to the tail of the stacker. His teeth shone like a negro's out of his dust-blackened face and his shirt was wet with sweat, but he motioned for "more straw" and David, accepting the*

Chaff filled the air during a demonstration of traditional threshing techniques at Old World Wisconsin in 1986. The living museum is a state historical site, featuring farms and rural living from various ethnic groups settling in the state. *Courtesy of Jim Brozek.*

*challenge, signaled for more speed. Frank swung his lash and yelled at the straining horses, the sleepy growl of the cylinder rose to a howl and the wheat came pulsing out at the spout in such a stream that the carriers were forced to trot on their path to and from the granary in order to keep the grain from piling up around the measurer. There was kind of splendid rivalry in this backbreaking toil—for each sack weighed ninety pounds.*[14]

# WISCONSIN'S QUALITY GINSENG FAVORED ON WORLD MARKET

Wisconsin ginseng is known worldwide as the purest, highest-quality ginseng. *Panax quinquefolius*, better known as American ginseng, is a white root with medicinal properties relieving stress, increasing stamina and boosting resistance to common illnesses such as colds.

The Ginseng Board of Wisconsin (GBW) was established in 1986 as a nonprofit organization representing the nearly two hundred Wisconsin ginseng growers. The GBW is funded through a mandatory assessment of ginseng acreage under shade.

The GBW is managed by an elected board of seven ginseng producers and functions under a marketing order managed by the Wisconsin Department of Agriculture, Trade & Consumer Protection. The GBW is the originator and owner of the Wisconsin Ginseng Seal. This trademark was developed in 1991 to protect the integrity of Wisconsin ginseng products.

The Wisconsin Ginseng Seal provides consumers with a simple, convenient method of identifying authentic Wisconsin ginseng at the point of purchase. Packaged products bearing the official Wisconsin Seal must contain 100 percent pure Wisconsin ginseng, grown and harvested in the state.

American ginseng has been cultivated in Wisconsin for more than a century, dating back to the 1800s. Today, Wisconsin farmers account for 96 percent of the country's total cultivated ginseng production.

The Fromm brothers of Hamburg were the first Wisconsin farmers to grow cultivated ginseng. In the 1930s, theirs was the largest commercial fur farm in the world, known as the home of the "million dollar foxes" after the New York Auction Company wrote a $1.3 million check for their fox pelts in 1929. After losing one-third of their foxes to disease, the Fromms invested $1 million and hired a researcher who developed a distemper vaccine that is still used in animals today. In 1934, they built a 5,600-square-foot house to entertain what they called "the world's most elite guests." This clubhouse can be toured in its original condition, including an original 1935 Brunswick four-lane bowling alley.

The Fromms used their profitable crop of ginseng to fund their fur business, transplanting one hundred wild ginseng plants from nearby forests to their own plots. Since that time, central Wisconsin has been the center of the United States cultivated ginseng trade. Many others soon replicated the process and began commercial production of ginseng, so that in the early 1900s, numerous ginseng farms existed in Wisconsin.

In 1919, Wisconsin became the leading ginseng-producing state, and by 1920, ginseng farms were found in almost all Wisconsin counties. Unlike other states, Wisconsin maintained ginseng production during the Second World War, and its dominance continued after that time. In 1954, out of the twenty-one acres of cultivated ginseng in the United States, twenty were in Wisconsin.

A variety of Wisconsin ginseng roots and products are available directly from the Ginseng and Herb Cooperative, including roots, tea cut ginseng, ginseng powder, capsules, chewing gum and other products.

The sensitive crop is grown in mounds to keep it dry and is shaded under canopies. It takes four years for ginseng plants to mature, and once they're harvested, the land can never be used for it again. Most of the crop's buyers are from China and Taiwan. The retail price of Wisconsin cultivated ginseng ranges from $30 to $120 or even reaching $300 per pound, much higher than the export price for dry roots, which ranges from $15 to $40 per pound.

In 1995, there were 1,468 ginseng growers in Wisconsin, but by 2006 there were only 190. There are a variety of reasons, such as increased competition from Canada and China, lack of marketing efforts in Asia and price depression due to counterfeit ginseng using

Inspectors look over a shaded ginseng crop in the early days of cultivation in Wisconsin. *Courtesy of the Ginseng Board of Wisconsin.*

the Wisconsin Ginseng Seal. The amount of ginseng under shade in 2011 was roughly 1,475 acres. This includes one-year, two-year, three-year and four-year-old crops.[15]

## COMMERCIAL FORESTRY

Wisconsin's commercial forests cover about 14.5 million acres, about 43 percent of the land area of the state. Forest-dependent industries are the second-largest manufacturer in the Wisconsin.

Although early explorers knew that the region's timberland presented opportunities of unlimited wealth, by the early 1860s, logging was proceeding at such a rapid pace that concerned citizens reported to the legislature on the "disastrous effects of destruction of forest trees now going on so rapidly." The first professional estimate of the effects of logging on the state came in 1898 with a report by Filibert Roth of the United States Department of Agriculture that

William Arnon (W.A.) Henry (1850–1932) was the first dean of University of Wisconsin College of Agriculture and Life Sciences and helped found the state's agricultural experimental station. He also established the university's one- and two-year Farm and Industry Short Course (FISC) program, geared to high school graduates interested in farming or another agricultural industry such as crop and soil management and the landscape industry. In 1898, Henry published a 661-page volume on stock feeding entitled *Feeds and Feeding: A Hand Book for the Student and Stockman. Courtesy of the University of Wisconsn–Madison Archives, no. SO7780.*

was submitted to the state's Forestry Commission. That agency had been established in 1897.

In 1903, the Wisconsin Forestry Commission was set up, with numerous University of Wisconsin researchers and academics on its board. Among them were College of Agriculture deans William Arnon (W.A.) and Henry and H.L. Russell. However, the commission was dismantled in 1915 and a new Conservation Commission set up with a division of forestry. In 1927, the commission was reorganized into a state department, which then evolved into the current Department of Natural Resources.

Two major steps toward managing the state forest resources were the passage of the forest crop law for private and county forests in 1927 and zoning legislation in 1929. These bills helped create a basis for forestry research and education that goes back to pioneer scientist Increase A. Lapham. In 1867, he had suggested a bill that would include advising on scientific experiments to learn the best methods for growing and managing forest trees.[16]

# A NORWEGIAN TELLS OF LIFE IN WISCONSIN

Anders Jensen Stortroen, an émigré from Norway in the 1850s, had been in America ten months, traveling throughout Illinois and Wisconsin. He reported on his travels to friends and family about the wonderful life on the farming frontier. The following is an excerpt from one of his letters written in 1853 from a stopover in Martell Township, Wisconsin:

> We first will tell you about the country, and we can say at once that it is a very fertile land, as one can sow almost what kind of seed he chooses, and he will be certain that it comes up, and just as certain that it will not freeze down again. Neither is there any trouble with fertilizing for any of farming, as it is unnecessary. Here the land is uniformly level except for small hills and valleys, so one place looks like another wherever one goes. In this locality, the water is as wholesome and good as in Norway, there being no difference. But as far as the woods are concerned, they are

*unpraiseworthy, since here no trees but oaks can be found, and they are not very plentiful on the farms the Norwegians have bought lately; but some of the Americans who settled here first have much woods and of the best quality, and they naturally did not settle in the poorest places. For they found both the most convenient locations and the best forests.*

*...meadows bear large crops, yes, fully as large as the luxuriant grass in Norway. Still, some of the Americans broke up land and seeded timothy seed which gives extremely high yields, and which is the best and most nourishing hay crop here also. What we call a "gaard" in Norway is called a farm here, and a large farm here consists of a dwelling house, a cellar and a stable. And here can be found many who have lived in American three or four years who do not yet have any house but live in cellars dug in the ground. Fine houses are built mostly of timbers (logs), but they not bevel the logs as in Norway, but they let the logs lie as they first fall, then they take stones or whatever is most convenient and chink between the logs, later working together clay and lime and plastering the walls, and with that they are ready. And the roofs of the houses are of boards, since here neither birch bark, sod or stone (slate) are used for roofs. Some of the Americans have houses which are built of sawed lumber, which are large and fine...*

*Here may be found all sorts of animals...two horses here, six or seven years old, cost from $25 to $30; two oxen four or five years old cost from $75 to $100; a cow from $20 to $30, and the cows milk a little more here than in Norway as a rule, and the milk is also just as good here as there. A four-wheeled wagon costs from $70 to $90, a plow costs from $12 to $18, a harrow from $4 to $8. A bushel wheat costs 50 cents, a bushel corn (maize) 25 cents, a bushel oats 15 cents, a bushel potatoes, 12½ cents. We have not see rye or barley.*

*One pound butter costs 10 cents, one pound pork 8 cents, one pound coffee 16 cents, one pound sugar 15 cents, one pound tobacco 40 cents, a pot of whiskey 12 cents...A pair of boots costs $5, a pair of shoes $2, one pair of trousers of wool and cotton cloth, $3, a coat of the same cloth $5. More need not be mentioned.*[17]

# NEED FOR EQUIPMENT

Glenn Pound, dean of the University of Wisconsin College of Agriculture, was always good for a quote when it came to agricultural studies and the importance of farming:

> *When I first came to Wisconsin, planting corn was quite an ordeal. Weather was often rainy, many times farmers got into the situation of being late planting, of getting his corn in. Well, now the farmer has learned he can buy heavy enough equipment so that all he has to do is wait for good weather and he can sweep though and get his corn in. The farmer has decided that that's in his economic interest to have that kind of equipment. In order to make it economic, he gets his operation large enough [to] make it that way. But that's not college research.*[18]

An Amish farmer in Wisconsin still tills his crops the old-fashioned, horse-drawn way. *Courtesy of Jim Brozek.*

## MAKING FARMSTEAD CHEESE

Anne Topham, considered a pioneer of making French-style chèvre in Wisconsin, has been making farmstead goat cheese at Fantome Farm for twenty years. She and Judy Borree moved to Wisconsin from Iowa and bought a fifty-acre farm that sits high on a hill forty miles west of Madison. With the help of friends, they built a barn for the goats and converted a garage into a small cheese factory they call a "cheeserie."

At Fantome Farm, Topham and Borree handcraft cheese in small batches with milk from about a dozen goats. It's not found at retail outlets, but you can see the two cheesemakers every Saturday during the growing season at the Madison farmers' market on Capitol Square. Their deliciously delicate chèvre is made with pasteurized milk from their own herd. It's occasionally marinated and herbed, as well provides a base for their Thyme Logs, which are dusted with herbs and cave aged for one to two weeks.

They also make small quantities of Boulot, a raw milk semihard cheese that's aged for four to six months. Another new cheese is the farm's award-winning Fleuri, a round cave-aged cheese dusted with clean ash. This cheese, based on a variety Topham and Borree discovered in France, won second place at the 2006 American Cheese Society competition.[19]

Cheesemaker Jim Meives of the Chula Vista Cheese Company proudly wears his "Dangerously Cheesy" T-shirt at the farmers' market on Madison's Capitol Square. *Courtesy of the author.*

# RISE OF ORGANIC FARMING

The 2008 USDA Organic Agriculture Census ranked Wisconsin second in the United States in the total number of organic farms. The census reported 2,714 organic farms in top-ranked California, with 1,222 organic farms in Wisconsin. The state leads the nation in the number of organic beef and dairy farms and ranks first for farms raising organic hogs, layer chickens and turkeys.

The state has experienced dramatic growth in organic agriculture since the National Organic Program was enacted in 2002. The

Wisconsinites love their organic produce, seeking out top-quality vegetables at outdoor markets around the state. *Courtesy of the author.*

number of organic farms in Wisconsin grew 157 percent from 2002 to 2007. The 2008 census also showed significant sales of organic agricultural products in Wisconsin. The state ranks sixth in the nation for total organic product sales, at $132.8 million, capturing 4.1 percent of total organic sales in the United States.

Wisconsin ranks second in the nation for organic milk sales, with its $85 million in sales representing 11.4 percent of the country's total. Milk from cows accounts for 64 percent of sales of organic farm products in Wisconsin. The state is first in

Pickled mushrooms are temptingly displayed at the farmers' market on Madison's Capitol Square. *Courtesy of the author.*

the number of farms raising organic field crops such as corn, oats, barley, winter wheat, hay and silage.

Organic processing, which adds value to the organic meat, milk and produce raised in Wisconsin, is also important. A 2011 survey by the Wisconsin Department of Agriculture, Trade and Consumer Protection indicated that gross income for Wisconsin organic processors ranged from more than $100 million to under $10,000.[20]

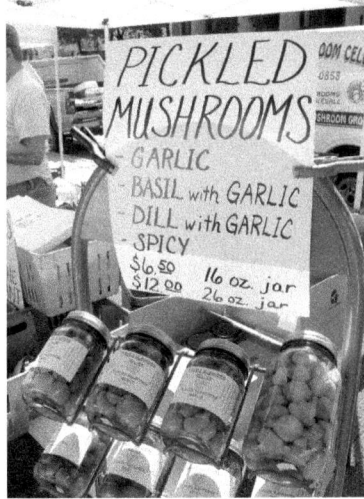

## A PUMPKIN TO BE PROUD OF

In 2010, Guinness World Records confirmed that a Wisconsin pumpkin was officially the world's heaviest. The gourd grown by Chris Stevens of New Richmond tipped the scales at 1,810.5 pounds, making it 85.0 pounds heavier than the previous record, a 1,725.0-pound pumpkin grown the previous year in Ohio. Stevens's pumpkin had a circumference of 186.5 inches, or more than fifteen

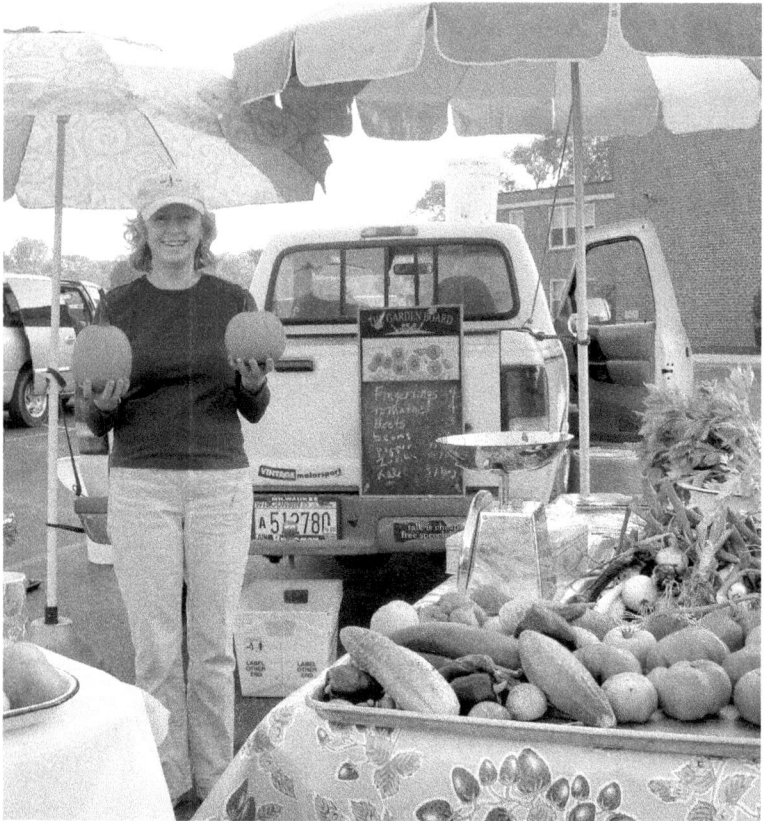

Pam Percy of Pampered Produce supplies vegetables to more than twenty Community Shared Agriculture (CSA) clients, as well as provides eggs and vegetables to restaurants and farmers' markets. Her urban acreage is the last remaining working farm in northern Milwaukee County. Percy has been raising chickens for eggs for almost thirty years. *Courtesy of the author.*

feet. Turned on its side, the pumpkin was more than waist-high to an average-size person. He attributed the massive veggie to a mixture of sunshine, rain, cow manure, fish emulsion and seaweed.[21]

# The Products

*Farming is a way of living, as well as a way of making a living.*
*—Chris Christensen*[1]

## CHEESE PLANTS MULTIPLY

At the annual meeting of the State Agricultural Society in February 1870, it was reported that there had been "scarcely less than 50 factories in operation" in 1869, and seventy-seven factories were listed by name in the Annual Report of the Society for 1870. Twenty of these were in Kenosha County, eight in Fond du Lac County, eight in Sheboygan County and from one to six in Dane, Dodge, Grant, Green, Green Lake, Jefferson, Lafayette, La Crosse, Monroe, Outagamie, Richland, Rock, Sauk, Walworth and Waukesha Counties. The Cold Spring Factory alone produced 191,000 pounds of cheese that year and the factory at Ladoga only 5,000 pounds less.[2]

## CHOICE FARMING LANDS FOR SALE

In 1903, plenty of land was still available for sale in Wisconsin, as seen in this newspaper advertisement of the day:

> *The John Arpin Lumber Company has 90,000 acres of choice farming lands for sale in the counties of Wood, Gates, Barron and Sawyer. They have a large saw mill plant with logging railroad at Atlanta, near Bruce on the Soo Line, where they offer extra inducements for settlers in the shape of cheap lands and a desirable market for labor and all the products of the soil.*
>
> *For prices and pamphlet write, John Arpin Lumber Co., Grand Rapids, Wisconsin.*[3]

A tray of juicy heritage tomatoes is showcased at the Fox Point Farmer's Market. *Courtesy of the author.*

## "Forest Town" Advocate

A thoughtful advocate of forest-farm communities in Wisconsin was R.B. Goodman, a lumberman and member of the State Conservation Commission in the 1930s. Goodman envisioned "forest towns," which would replace both ghostlike "sawmill towns" and the "wilderness slums" of scattered stump farmers. These towns would be more compact than existing farm settlements but less compact than sawmill towns. The residents would be permanent settlers, not transitory as in sawmill towns. They would work in conservation and harvesting of timber while being "part-time subsistence farmers." Goodman put his ideas to work on his timberlands in northeastern Wisconsin.

By 1944, he reported that three thousand people formed a "working circle" within a ten-mile radius of the village of Goodman in northwestern Marinette County. "Employment in the Goodman working circle," he explained, "is almost equally divided between farming and the forest industries," which were based on sustained-yield forestry. "More acreage is put into crops each year," he emphasized. This was possible because "mill employment provides for extended leaves of absence for farm planting and the harvesting of crops. In the woods, peak employment is during the winter months."[4]

## Take Some Diastoid and Call Me in the Morning

Originally developed as a nutritional supplement for infants and people with bad digestion, malted milk changed how Americans ate. Pharmacist James Horlick fine-tuned his wheat- and malt-based drink in London but moved to Racine, Wisconsin, to link up his brother, William. The two formed a company in 1873 to produce baby food. Ten years later, the Horlicks patented their formula that they marketed under the name "diastoid." The name didn't register with purchasers, so the company trademarked the name "malted milk" in 1887. The Horlicks' high-calorie invention found many admirers, such as explorers like Admiral Richard Byrd, who appreciated the convenience and its light weight, as well as it being nonperishable.[5]

# 1920s FARM POPULATION DROPS

Wisconsin's farm population dropped dramatically during the 1920s, declining from 35 to 30 percent of the population. Farm income in the state had peaked at $549 million in 1919 but plummeted to $320 million in 1921. It recovered slowly to $439 million in 1929 when the Great Depression occurred. During World War I, the federal government had intervened to set livestock and milk prices, so farmers felt that they were encouraged to increase productivity. But with the decrease in supports after the war, many farmers were stuck with huge bills for equipment, land and property

In about 1928, the Muehl family picked vegetables on their Racine County farm to sell during the era's hard economic times. *From left to right*: Marvin, Marion, Walter, Blanche and Elaine. *Courtesy of the Waterford Public Library.*

improvements. They had to pay higher prices, along with higher taxes due to postwar inflation. Milk receipts in 1922 were only two-thirds of what they had been two years previously, and hog prices were halved.

It was time to get off the farm, with the 1920 census showing that the urban population had increased 23.9 percent over the previous decade, while farm numbers increased only 4.4 percent.[6]

## DAIRY MAN

John LeFeber owned the Gridley Dairy Company at 138 Eighth Street, Milwaukee, and was a key player in organizing the Milwaukee Milk Producers' Association. LeFeber also helped develop a cooperative marketing program for the state's many dairy products in the early 1900s. LeFeber was born on February 1, 1863, on the Alexander Mitchell farm, where his father, Jozias, was the manager. Mitchell was a Wisconsin entrepreneur who built the Milwaukee Road and was grandfather to noted war hero General Billy Mitchell. LeFeber was also chairman of the Fluid Milk Committee under Herbert Hoover's Food Conservation Administration during World War I and was two-term president of the International Milk Dealers Association, which he helped form in 1907.

He started dairying in 1886 when he purchased a herd of 110 milk cows, 8 horses, two milk routes and the farm machinery on his 165-acre property. The purchase was made entirely on credit, based on the observation of young LeFeber's character by the farmer who made the sale. Within eight years, he had repaid the loan, increased his herd and added a third milk route. In 1903, through the merger of several small companies, LeFeber became president of a milk distributing business of eighteen routes, forming the basis of the Gridley Dairy Company. He was president of the firm for the next twenty-eight years, eventually supplying milk to almost 75 percent of the city of Milwaukee and its suburbs. The firm employed more than one thousand workers. LeFeber was the first milk distributor to sell bottled milk west of New York City, a move initially resisted because Milwaukee housewives were accustomed to buying milk in bulk.

LeFeber was a charter member of the Milwaukee Rotary Club, formalized in 1913. In addition to leading tours of his dairy for his fellow Rotarians, he was a strong promoter of anything related to the Wisconsin dairy industry, as evidenced here from the organization's minutes of May 16, 1918:

> *Owing to the courtesy of Rotarian LeFeber who, as you are aware, has devoted a great part of his time to Government work connected with the war we shall be honored by the presence of Miss Edna Randall of the Department of Agriculture of Washington. She will give a four-minute talk on the uses to which skimmed milk can be applied and will especially demonstrate the qualities of cottage cheese. It is felt that every Rotarian will be interested in the work of the Government in various food products.*[7]

# THE PINERY

Carl Penskover of Rice Lake reminisced about his days growing up in northern Wisconsin throughout the 1910s and 1920s:

> *The men would go into the woods* [to cut timber] *in the fall, then come back in the spring with their money…and that was the only means of getting any money, really…there wasn't much dairy in them days. You never milked in the wintertime…when I was a kid anyway.*[8]

# DIGGING POTATOES

Even in 1900, it helped to have the proper equipment:

> *Indications point to a large potato crop this season and the question of economically harvesting the crop is receiving the consideration of the planters. Large growers know that to produce potatoes at a low cost, the harvesting must be done by machinery and many*

A harvest crew at the Prosser farm worked the potato fields in Antigo, circa 1950. *Courtesy of the Wisconsin Potato & Vegetable Growers Association.*

*small growers and general farms have also found it profitable to use a potato digger.*

*Among the best machines designed for this purpose is the Hoover Potato Digger, manufactured by Hoover, Prout & Com, Avery, Ohio. Any reader of the Agriculturist having an acre of potatoes to dig this fall should write to them for their illustrated catalogue and prices.*[9]

## POTATOES OVER THE YEARS

Wisconsin Potato & Vegetable Growers communications director Tamas Houlihan reviewed the organization's sixty-year existence in his essay "Full Spud Ahead":

*The year was 1948. An average yield of potatoes was 96 hundred weight (cwt.) per acre. As a state, Wisconsin growers raised 78,000 acres for a total production of 7,488,000 cwt.*

Penelope Potato (Lori Gunderson) poses with Miss Tator Tot Lauren Rine (right) and her little sister, Rachel. *Courtesy of the Wisconsin Potato & Vegetable Growers Association.*

Fast-forward to 2008, the sixtieth anniversary year of the Wisconsin Potato & Vegetable Growers Association. The average yield of potatoes was about 440 cwt. per acre. Wisconsin growers raised 65,000 acres for a total production of 28,600,000 cwt. Portage County alone raised between eight and nine million cwt. each year.

Times have certainly changed. The state's production has nearly quadrupled, while acreage has actually declined by 17%. One obvious trend is that the number of growers has decreased significantly, while the size of the farms has increased dramatically. The mom and pop farms of the past have been replaced by large multi-faceted growing operations, although many are still considered to be "family farms," run by third and fourth generation growers.

One constant over the past sixty years has been the contributions of an organization formed by potato growers for potato growers. "The Potato Growers of Wisconsin" was founded on February 13, 1948. The Association was set up as a non-profit organization, to organize the potato growers and handlers of the state; to promote and protect their interests; and to arrange, hold and conduct meetings of potato growers and potato handlers in the state. The name changed in 1952 to Wisconsin Potato Growers Association, Inc., and then again in 1964 to the Wisconsin Potato & Vegetable Growers Association, Inc.

The original group who signed the articles of incorporation included: B.H. (Ben) Diercks of Antigo; Felix Zeloski of Antigo; Barron West of Sarona; Robert Erickson of Waupaca; James D. Swan, Jr. of Delavan; and Luke Kuczmarski of Rhinelander. The first regular meeting of the association was held on March 20, 1948, in Stevens Point.[10]

# ESTABLISHMENT OF FIRST DAIRY BOARD

In 1871, the Marschall Dairy Laboratory retold the founding of the Wisconsin cheese board:

*The year 1871 found the market glutted and the price of cheese went down to eight cents per pound. This situation led to the establishment the following year of the first Dairy Board in the State by a group of dairymen in Jefferson County. Merchants in Milwaukee and Chicago as well as cheesemakers throughout the State were invited to attend the first market day at Watertown. The commission men came but, from the outset, discouraged the enterprise and few actual sales were effected on the Board.*

The next year, a dairy board of trade was formed at Sheboygan Falls by the Sheboygan County Dairymen's Association; 226 tons of the total of 573 tons of cheese made in the county that year was offered on the board and a goodly proportion of cash sales resulted, the price received averaging about ten cents a pound.

By this time, Wisconsin cheese had found its way to New York and across the seas to London and Liverpool where it had made a favorable impression. This led to attempts to deal direct with the English buyers, and in the winter of 1873, C.H. Wilder, who was operating a factory at Evansville, decided to visit the British cheese markets. With him went four carloads of cheese from his factory that he proposed to market upon his arrival. He succeeded in doing this to his satisfaction and returned with the report that there was an excellent opportunity for Wisconsin dairymen to market in this fashion.[11]

# CHEESEMAKERS SIGN THEIR CONSTITUTION

The minutes of a meeting of the Wisconsin Dairymen's Association in 1872 covered a lot of ground, with conversations ranging from prices to shipping:

*President* [Chester] *Hagen then made some very interesting remarks, upon the kinds of cheese and other qualifications demanded by the various markets in the United States. St. Louis wanted a soft cheese, weighing about 60 lbs. The New York*

The Products

There's nothing like hot Wisconsin cheese for a different tasty treat, a gooey staple at the Wisconsin State Fair. *Courtesy of the author.*

*market, called for a harder cheese, slightly colored. J.C. Hull said that Davis Bros. in Chicago had stated to him in a recent conversation that cheese made in a thirteen-inch hoop would give better satisfaction in that market. Mr. S. Barrett, of Juneau, stated that in the Liverpool market, cheese made in a fourteen-inch hoop, weighing about 50 lbs. would bring ½ cent more per lb. Remarks were offered upon this and kindred subjects, by various gentlemen present.*

133

*The subject of the central market like that of Little Falls, New York, was then discussed, and R.F. Dousman, offered the following resolution, which was adopted:*

*Resolution: That the Executive Committee be directed to appoint two days each month, in which a butter and cheese market shall be held in some convenient building, in Watertown, and to make all necessary arrangements therefor.*

*Mr. Hazen stated that last summer, he shipped a quantity of cheese to New York by the carload with satisfactory results. By the arrangements growing out of a combination resulting from the formation of a State Association, he thought much better results even could be obtained. Mr. Dousman informed the Convention, that last summer, he shipped June cheese to Liverpool, which reached their destination thirty days from time of shipment. The freight cost one cent per pound, in gold, and the commissions and other expenses one cent more. The cheese netted ten cents per pound. He thought this exceeded any sale he had heard of for June made cheese. Mr. Drake offered the following resolution, which was adopted:*

*Resolved—That the Secretary of this Association, be directed to notify as far as possible, all regular cheese buyers and commission men throughout the Northwest, and also of the cheese factory men in the State of Wisconsin, and all members of this Association, on what days the markets will be held.*

*After varied discussions upon subjects connected with the dairy interests and the signing of the Constitution by over 20 members, the Association adjourned to meet at the Linden House, on Thursday, March 7th, at 2 o'clock p.m.—W.D. Hoard, Sec'y. Lake Mills.*[12]

# PROFESSOR POUND LOVED COWS

Glenn S. Pound was the seventh dean of the University of Wisconsin College of Agriculture, serving from 1964 to 1979. He had authored more than one hundred technical research papers and was

Glenn Pound, dean, University of
Wisconsin College of Agriculture
and Life Sciences, 1964–2010.
*Courtesy of the University of Wisconsin–
Madison Archives, no. SO7777.*

active in numerous professional organizations, traveling around the world and evaluating agricultural methods and education.

He was fond of saying that the "dairy cow means more to human welfare than any other animal, save man himself. We would be far better off as a people to forego many of the aspects of our affluent life than to let…its products become of less importance."

He advocated that proceeds from a tax on oleomargarine be appropriated to the building of a new animal sciences building at the university. The sale of such a product, however, had been outlawed since 1895 to protect the dairy industry. Yet Wisconsinites regularly had flaunted the law, often buying margarine out of state.

The pressure to repeal that ban grew in the 1960s as Wisconsin was left as the only state with the prohibition. Residents were getting around the law by buying margarine in neighboring states just across the border.

Then state senator Martin Schreiber, a twenty-six-year-old Democrat who went on to serve as acting governor in the 1970s, proposed doing away with the ban in 1965, but he said that rural Republicans bottled it up. So he came up with a creative way to make his case: a blind taste test.

One of butter's most ardent supporters, Republican senator Gordon Roseleip, happily took the taste test and promptly chose margarine as better tasting. His flub made national news.

"That was the beginning of the end," Schreiber said.

It wasn't until after his death in 1989 that Roseleip's family members said that they had been secretly going to Iowa for years to buy margarine, where it was legal to feed it to Roseleip instead of butter out of concerns for his health. In 1967, the state ban on such sales was repealed.

> *People do things for different reasons. Wisconsin had for over 75 years tried to protect its butter industry by a legal ban against the sale of colored margarine. The support of a bill to legalize the sale of colored margarine by certain agricultural leaders was not given to support margarine sales but because they thought margarine's time had come. They believe that the creation of a new research facility would give the greatest protection of the future of the dairy industry. How right they were. Who among us today believes that the ban against margarine could have survived the thrusts of Naderism and consumerism of the past four years? I dare say none.*[13]

# TOUGH TIMES LEAD TO CORPORATE OFFICE

Gustav E. Strandt, president and general manager of the Milwaukee Dairy & Supply Company, is identified with an industry that has been one of the chief factors in bringing Milwaukee into commercial prominence and making it known throughout the world as the Cream City. He grew up on his family farm near Cedarburg, Wisconsin, "and the urge of necessity prompted him early to take his place as a factor in the work of the fields, assisting in the early spring planting and in the cultivation of the fields until crops were gathered in the late autumn, having little time to attend school."

When he was twelve years, Strandt began working in the Cedarburg Woolen Mill for thirty-two cents per day, his day's work covering ten hours. He worked there for two years, and at the age of sixteen, he "left the parental roof with a cash capital of sixty-five cents. Already he had had considerable experience in the business world and had developed self-reliance and industry far beyond that attributed to most lads of his years. Making his way to Milwaukee, he paid fifty cents of his precious capital for his railroad fare and had in his possession but fifteen cents when he reached his destination."

He quickly landed a job with the Rockwell Planing Mill at five dollars per week and eventually moved on to work at the Cream City Planing Mill. In the meantime, he was experimenting with patents. By the time he was eighteen, Stradt was "displaying much skill and ingenuity."

> *It was at that time that he organized the Cedarburg Milk Company and for fifteen years was engaged in the business. During this entire period, he continued his experimenting on dairy machinery and has produced many styles of dairy machines, which he did not put upon the market, however, for lack of funds. He patented what is known as the Milwaukee sanitary bottle filler and capper, which has become known all over the world and was the first rotary milk bottle filler and capper invented. Many firms have attempted to imitate this but such a course is an infringement on Mr. Strandt's rights.*
>
> *Mr. Strandt had no path of roses before him. He encountered obstacles and difficulties which would have discouraged many a man of less resolute spirit but perseverance, courage and determination enabled him to continue on his way. He labored night and day to get his patent completed, selling his home for funds and borrowing money from his friends but in the end he has won the victory and is now enjoying the success of his inventions. Today, the company of which he is the head has a large factory with modern buildings and is doing an excellent business, while its goods are sent to all parts of America, also to England, Japan, China, Canada, Australia, South America, Panama and other lands. Mr. Strandt has given his entire time to his business, having little leisure for social activities.*

He and his wife, Dora, adopted four children and served on the board of the Bethany Lutheran Church. "His entire career has been actuated by devotion to high ideals and to a notable sense of duty and what he has accomplished is the direct result of capability, guided by intelligence and by the highest principles of integrity and honor."[14]

## WISCONSIN MILK PRODUCTION SOARS

*Wisconsin's production of milk is ten tons for every minute of the day and night throughout the year. One tenth of the nation's total milk supply! Every pound of this health and strength giving fluid is a symbol of good roads, good school and happy homes everywhere. On Wisconsin!*[15]

## GETTING CANNED

Milwaukee Rotarians were encouraged to be present with a "good appetite" at a luncheon of canned food on March 4, 1924, in the Elizabethan Room of the Milwaukee Athletic Club:

> *Next week is National Canned Food Week, and…the luncheon will be a very unusual one, and every item on the menu will be made of an appetizing article that can be purchased in cans. Our speaker will be Mr. W.E. Nicholoy, business secretary of the Wisconsin Pea Canners Association. He will tell us some interesting facts regarding the canned food industry, which has grown into enormous proportions in the United States.*

Death's Door Vodka, made from Washington Island wheat, is a Wisconsin-made product finding favor among drinkers around the country. *Courtesy of the author.*

The organization's meeting on March 11 of that year featured T.H. Campion, superintendent of the Milwaukee County School of Agriculture and Domestic Economy, talking about "the wonderful strides made in the agricultural line to assist the farmers."[16]

Leah Caplan helped kick-start the wheat industry on Door County's Washington Island when she opened her Washington Hotel, Restaurant and Culinary School. The lack of viable markets for the wheat almost spelled the end for the island's farmers, but Caplan's use of the crop for her baked products revived the industry. In 2009, she began developing recipes and providing shopper education for Metcalfe's Markets, several gourmet-style stores that highlighted local, organic foods in Madison. Caplan was a founding board member of Slow Food Madison and Home Grown Wisconsin, a farmers' cooperative. *Courtesy of the author.*

# UNIVERSITY AIDS WAR EFFORT

Following the entry of the United States into World War I, the University of Wisconsin's College of Agriculture thrust itself into the war effort. The governing slogan at the college was "Food Will Win the War." The university's Cooperative Extension became the focal point for these efforts. In the spring of 1917, Dean H.L. Russell wrote that "with the active entrance of America into the war, it was apparent that the first duty of the Agricultural College lay in the stimulation of production, and immediately the extension activities were directed toward this end."

Among the many projects that Dean Russell explained were contained under these headings: Insuring the Corn Crop, Bread Grain Drive, Distribution of Seed Potatoes, Vigorous Campaign Increases Silo Construction, Fighting Plant Diseases, Land Clearing Aids Food Production, Return of the Sheep Industry to Wisconsin, War Garden Campaigning, Junior Workers Help Increase Food Supplies, Redistribution of Live Stock, Pork Production, Food Conservation Proves Popular, Increase Production Through Drainage and Inoculation Increases Legume Crops.[17]

# FERTILIZING THE ORCHARD

A 1903 *Wisconsin Agriculturist* newspaper offered excellent tips on manuring an orchard that are still viable:

> *In the endeavor to fertilize the orchard by plowing under green crops, it should be remember that little will be accomplished unless nitrogen-gathering crops are used. Oats, millet, rye, timothy or corn, turned under, will only give back to the soil what has been taken from it to produce the crop. But if clovers, peas, soy beans or vetches are sown and plowed under, fertility will be added, as these crops all draw nitrogen from the air during their growth.*
>
> *Green manuring is all right for young orchards if proper care is exercised not to interfere with the root growth in plowing. It is also*

*good for old orchards. But nothing is any better than an occasional dressing of barnyard manure. Some kind of fertilization is necessary if fruit is expected to be in abundance.*[18]

# MEASURING FAT CONTENT IN MILK

In 1890, the College of Agriculture at the University of Wisconsin was about one year old. In that year, Stephen Moulton Babcock (1843–1931), professor of agricultural chemistry, had perfected an inexpensive test to determine the amount of butterfat in milk. The Babcock Test was quickly taken up by farmers all around the world because they could discover and document the precise composition of their product. It helped raise dairying from an agriculture sidelight to an efficient scientific discipline. The following is from Babcock's first report on the project:

> *During the past few years, a number of methods have been proposed by which the estimation of fat in milk may be accomplished without the delicate appliances of a chemical laboratory, and by persons unskilled in chemical manipulations. Although most of these methods have been found either too complicated or too expensive to meet the wants of the practical dairyman, a few of them are being used to a considerable extent by careful breeders of dairy stock to determine the quality of their cows, and by creameries for adjusting the price of milk between their patrons…*
>
> *The chief obstacle to this much desired end, at present, is the time required and the expense involved for apparatus and chemicals where a large number of tests must be made from day to day…Whether this test will find a place among those already introduced, time alone can decide. In the hope that it may benefit some who are striving to improve their stock and enable creameries to avoid the evil of the present system, the test is given to the public.*[19]

# WISCONSIN WOODPILE

Forestry expert Hugh P. Baker, of the New York State College of Forestry at Syracuse University, discussed the state of the nation's timber industry at the Milwaukee Rotary Club in 1921. Baker went on to become president of the University of Massachusetts, writing numerous treatises on the lumber industry.

*The woodpile is the foundation of the paper industry, and our present task is the organization of the woodpile to meet the future of American industry. Wisconsin is one of the great papermaking districts in the United States, and so the woodpile is a Wisconsin problem. But the woodpile is more than a paper problem. Take Milwaukee's great industries, its car shops, box factories, any of its great plants, and think what would happen if the supply of wood were to be shut off.*

*…The answer to the problem is to make every acre not fit for agricultural crops produce trees. Make the loafing work. There are enough productive forest lands east of the Mississippi to give us forests which will not only produce all of the wood we need for the paper industry, but will make us a much greater export nation, as far as pulp wood is concerned, pulp and maker, than any other nation on earth.*[20]

# Notes

## The Land

1. From an address before the Wisconsin State Agricultural Society in Milwaukee, September 30, 1859, in "*Transactions of the Wisconsin State Agricultural Society, 1858–1859*," *Wisconsin Magazine of History 10, no. 3 (1926–27):* 287–99. Wisconsin Historical Society.
2. Schaefer, *History of Agriculture in Wisconsin*, 7.
3. Hintz, *Afterglow*, 7, 27–28.
4. *Wisconsin Agriculturist*, "Buying a Farm."
5. Current, *Wisconsin: A History*, 67–68.
6. Racine History, "Racine History Timeline, 1699–1899."
7. Lincoln, "Milwaukee Speech."
8. Moore, "Some Recorded Facts," 4.
9. Garland, *Daughter of the Middle Border*, 184.
10. Moore, "Some Recorded Facts," 10.
11. Schultz, *History of the Dairy Science Department*, 12.
12. Knopes, *Any Damn Fool Can Be a Farmer*, 11.
13. *Waukesha Daily Freeman*, "Farm for Sale."
14. Henry, "Biennial Board Report, 1902–1903," 67.
15. *Oshkosh Northwestern*, "Value of Farm Institutes."

16. Gard and Gard, *My Land, My Home, My Wisconsin*, 37.

17. Johnson, "It's Time to Put Down Roots in Crawford County," 31.

18. *Among Ourselves*, "Fund Established."

19. Wisconsin Farm Bureau membership brochure for Chris Christensen; *Seventy-five Years of Farm Bureau in Wisconsin*, 3; Wisconsin Farm Bureau Federation, "Founding of the Wisconsin Farm Bureau."

20. Pound, "U.S. Agriculture and World Food Needs," 17.

21. Hatch, "Agriculture's Triple Seal," 2.

22. Garland, *Son of the Middle Border*, 12.

23. University of Wisconsin Extension, "History of UW Extension."

24. Walters, "Devil-Wagon Days," 69–70.

25. Luther, "Farmers' Institutes in Wisconsin, 1885–1933," 60.

26. Austin, *Wisconsin Story*, 227.

27. College of Agricultural & Life Sciences, University of Wisconsin–Madison, "CALS History."

28. *Seventy-five Years of Farm Bureau in Wisconsin*, 19–20.

29. Upper, "With One Foot in the Furrow," 381.

30. Gard and Gard, *My Land, My Home, My Wisconsin*, 65.

31. *Creamery and Milk Plant Monthly*, "Creamery-Milk Plant News," 41.

32. Beck, "Wisconsin in the War of the Rebellion"; Garland, *Main Travelled Roads*, 169–70.

33. Hofacker, "Selling the Farm"; Smoot, *Farm Life*, 43.

34. Nesbit and Thompson, *Wisconsin*, 489; Schwarze, "1933 Clark County Milk Strike."

35. *Green Bay Press Gazette*, "Brown County Fair Opens"; Pagel, "Balloons, Big Races at 1909 County Fair," 30–31.

## *The People*

1. Coon, "The Ins and Outs of Tobacco Culture."

2. Smoot, *Farm Life*, 11.

3. Grough, *Farming the Cutover*, 228.

4. Radisson, *Early Native Peoples, Explorers, Traders, and Settlers.*

5. *Wisconsin Magazine of History* 18, no. 2, Documents and Gardner Letters (1934): 204–5; Baker, "Gardner Letters," Wisconsin Historical Collections, vi, 463–64.

6. Smoot, *Farm Life*, 20–23.

7. "Proceedings," Wisconsin Agricultural Society, date unknown; Gard and Gard, *My Land, My Home, My Wisconsin*, 61.

8. Russell, "Grandpa Russell's Own Story."

9. *Newsletter of the Civil War Round Table*, "General Orders No. 11-11," 6–7.

10. *Wisconsin Agriculturist*, "Benefits of Green County," 3.

11. Wikipedia, "Henry Cullen Adams"; Wisconsin Historical Society, "Henry Cullen Adams."

12. Smith, "Why I Am a Horticulturist"; Pagel, "Smith a Market Gardener—And More," 21.

13. Garland, *Rose of Dutcher's Coolly*, 24–25.

14. Williams and Marosy, *With One Foot in the Furrow*, 3.

15. Austin, *Wisconsin Story*, 230.

16. Austin, *Wisconsin Story*, 227.

17. Honeywell, "La Follette and His Legacy."

18. *Creamery and Milk Plant Monthly*, "Notices," 40.

19. Knopes, *Any Damn Fool Can Be a Farmer*, 7.

20. Austin, *Wisconsin Story*, 230; Olson, "National Farmers Organization Supports Bargaining Rights"; NFO news release, "National Farmers Organization."

21. Russell, *Among Ourselves*; Wikipedia, "Henry Wallace."

22. United States Department of Agriculture, *Agriculture Yearbook*, 1924, 1.

23. *Among Ourselves*, "Swiss Cheesemakers Dairy School."

24. Marschall Dairy Laboratory, "Cheesemaking in Wisconsin," 7, 29; Hintz, *Spirited History of Milwaukee Brews*, 7–9; Hintz and Percy, *Wisconsin Cheese*, 3; Wisconsin Cheese Information, "Join Us On a Tour of Wisconsin's Storied Cheesemaking Past."

25. Hintz and Percy, *Wisconsin Cheese*, 191.

26. Lemke Seed website.

27. Stone, "George Engelhardt," *Racine*, 39.

28. Hill and Smith, *Man in the "Cut-Over,"* 48–49.

29. Stone, "George Engelhardt," *Racine*, 451.

30. *Seventy-five Years of Farm Bureau in Wisconsin*, 14.

31. Russell, *Among Ourselves*.

32. *Seventy-five Years of Farm Bureau in Wisconsin*, 15–16; Wisconsin State Board of Agriculture, "Annual Report"; Reilly, "McKerrow Family History."

33. Zondag, "Address to Employees, Customers, Business Associates and Friends," 2; Burns, "Executive Q&A."
34. Smith, "Why I Am a Horticulturist"; Pagel, "Two Kinds of Farming," 20–21.
35. Alice in Dairyland website.
36. *Organic Broadcaster*, "2008 Farmers of the Year."
37. Hintz, *Afterglow*, 34–35.
38. Smoot, *Farm Life*, 27.

# *The Animals*

1. Gard and Gard, *My Land, My Home, My Wisconsin*, 54.
2. Ibid., 51.
3. Wisconsin Milk Marketing Board at Wisconsin Cheese Information website; Lone Acres Farm & Moraine Airedales, "A Few of Our Cows."
4. Hatch, "Organize for Dairy Marketing."
5. Pagel, "Holsteins at Home Here."
6. Dan Patch Historical Society website.
7. Faville, "History of the Cheese Industry in Wisconsin," 16.
8. Schaefer, *History of Agriculture in Wisconsin*, 126.
9. *Among Ourselves*, "Beef and Swine Exhibitions."
10. Schaefer, *History of Agriculture in Wisconsin*, 124.
11. Wisconsin State Cow Chip Throw and Festival website.
12. *Wisconsin Agriculturist*, "Breeding Mares," 7.
13. Schaefer, *History of Agriculture in Wisconsin*, 117–18.
14. Austin, *Wisconsin Story*, 238.
15. *The Rotarian*, "Items of Interest," 92.
16. *Wisconsin State Journal*, "Gov. Philipp Pays Tribute to Hoard."
17. Gard and Gard, *My Land, My Home, My Wisconsin*, 111.
18. Hatch, "Organize for Dairy Marketing," 10.
19. Schultz, *History of the Dairy Science Department*, 71; Andrews, "Patents: Breeding High-Volume Dairy Cows."
20. Wisconsin Dairy Goat Association website.
21. Hintz and Percy, *Wisconsin Cheese*, 118–19.
22. *Wisconsin Agriculturist*, "Judging Sows," 7.

# The Crops

1. Gard and Gard, *My Land, My Home, My Wisconsin*, 35.
2. Lincoln, "Milwaukee Speech."
3. Reaves, *Wisconsin*, 61.
4. Gorst Valley Hops website, "History of Wisconsin Hops"; Bohn, "Hop Cultural in Early Sauk County," 389.
5. Pagel, "Two Kinds of Farming," 9.
6. Reaves, *Wisconsin*, 39, 57.
7. Wisconsin State Cranberry Growers Association, "Cranberry Facts."
8. Knutsen and Meany, "Tobacco in Wisconsin."
9. Tobacco Institute, "A Chapter in America's Industrial Growth."
10. Ibid.
11. Winnebago County, Wisconsin County Agricultural Agent, "Annual Report," 6.
12. Clark County Internet Library Project, "Windstorm."
13. *History of Milwaukee*, vol. 3, 387.
14. Garland, *Son of the Middle Border*, 52–53.
15. Ginseng Board of Wisconsin, "About the Ginseng Board"; Cheng and Mitchell, "Status of the Wisconsin Ginseng Industry"; Fromm Bros. Historical Preservation Society website, "Fromm Brothers' Story."
16. Patton, "Forest Pathology," in *With One Foot in the Furrow*, 138–39.
17. Stortroen, letter from Martell Township; Fapso, *Norwegians in Wisconsin*, 57–59.
18. Pound, "There's No Turning Back."
19. Hintz and Percy, *Wisconsin Cheese*, 117–18.
20. Silva et al., "Organic Agriculture in Wisconsin."
21. *Huffington Post*, "World's Largest Pumpkin."

# The Products

1. Christensen, "What Place Has Culture in the Life of the Farmer?"; Jenkins, *A Centennial History*, 106.
2. Marschall Dairy Laboratory, "Cheesemaking in Wisconsin," 13, 15.
3. *Wisconsin Agriculturist*, "Choice Farm Land for Sale," 11.
4. Grough, *Farming the Cutover*, 183–84.
5. Wisconsin Historical Society website, "That's Meat and Drink to Me."

6. Nesbit and Thompson, *Wisconsin*, 459–60.

7. "John LeFeber, President of Wisconsin's Largest Milk Distributing Organization"; *Borden Eagle*, "John LeFeber"; Adkinson, "Meeting Minutes."

8. Smoot, *Farm Life*, 18.

9. *Wisconsin Agriculturist*, "Digging Potatoes," 5.

10. Houlihan, "Full Spud Ahead."

11. Marschall Dairy Laboratory, "Cheesemaking in Wisconsin," 21, 23.

12. Hoard, "Meeting Minutes," Wisconsin Dairymen's Association Convention, 5–7.

13. Pound, from a speech at the dedication of the University of Wisconsin Animal Sciences Building; Jenkins, *A Centennial History*, 163; *Wisconsin State Journal*, "Wisconsin Ban on Margarine."

14. *History of Milwaukee City and County*, vol. 3, "Gustav E. Strand," 19.

15. Hatch, "Organize for Dairy Marketing," 24.

16. Albenberg, Milwaukee Rotary Club meeting reminders, February 29 and March 7, 1924.

17. Russell, "Report of the Dean of the College of Agriculture." 119; Jenkins, *A Centennial History*, 73.

18. *Wisconsin Agriculturist*, "Fertilizing Orchards," 9.

19. Babcock, "A New Method," 4; Wisconsin History website, "The Babcock Test."

20. Baker, "The Woodpile."

# Bibliography

## *Books*

Austin, H. Russell. *The Wisconsin Story: The Building of a Vanguard State*. Milwaukee, WI: Milwaukee Journal, 1964.

Beck, J.D., ed. "Wisconsin in the War of the Rebellion." In *Wisconsin Blue Book*. Madison: Wisconsin Legislature, 1907.

Current, Richard Nelson. *Wisconsin: A History*. New York: W.W. Norton & Company, 1977.

Fapso, Richard J. *Norwegians in Wisconsin*. Madison: University of Wisconsin Press, 2001.

Gard, Robert, and Maryo Gard. *My Land, My Home, My Wisconsin*. Milwaukee, WI: Milwaukee Journal, 1978.

Garland, Hamlin. *Daughter of the Middle Border*. New York: MacMillan Company, 1921.

———. *Main Travelled Roads*. New York: Harper and Brothers Publishers, 1930.

———. *Rose of Dutcher's Coolly*. Lincoln: University of Nebraska Press. Bison Book edition reprinted from the 1895 edition published by Stone & Kimball, Chicago.

———. *Son of the Middle Border*. New York: MacMillan Company, 1914.

Grough, Robert. *Farming the Cutover: A Social History of Northern Wisconsin, 1900–1940*. Lawrence: University Press of Kansas, 1997.

Hachten, Harva, and Terese Allen. *The Flavor of Wisconsin: An Informal History of Food and Eating in the Badger State*. Wisconsin Historical Society Press. 2009. 392 pp.

Hintz, Martin. *Afterglow: The Story of a Farm*. Milwaukee, WI: circulated by the Uihlein family, 2010.

———. *A Spirited History of Milwaukee Brews and Booze*. Charleston, SC: The History Press, 2011.

Hintz, Martin, and Pam Percy. *Wisconsin Cheese: A Cookbook and Guide to the Cheeses of Wisconsin*. Guildford, CT: Three Forks Press/Globe Pequot, 2008.

*History of Milwaukee City and County*. Vol. 3. Chicago: S.J. Clarke Publishing Company, 1922.

Jenkins, John W. *A Centennial History: A History of the College of Agriculture and Life Sciences at the University of Wisconsin–Madison*. Madison: College of Agriculture and Life Sciences, University of Wisconsin–Madison, 1991.

Knopes, Bob. *Any Damn Fool Can Be a Farmer*. Middleton, WI: Badger Books, 2005.

Nesbit, Robert C., and William F. Thompson. *Wisconsin: A History*. Madison: University of Wisconsin Press, 1989.

Pagel, Ray. "Balloons, Big Races at 1909 County Fair." *Our Agricultural Heritage*. Green Bay, WI: Brown County Agricultural Bicentennial Committee, 1976.

———. "Holsteins at Home Here." *Our Agricultural Heritage*. Green Bay, WI: Brown County Agricultural Bicentennial Committee, 1976.

———. "Smith a Market Gardener—And More." *Our Agricultural Heritage*. Green Bay, WI: Brown County Agricultural Bicentennial Committee, 1976.

———. "Two Kinds of Farming." *Our Agricultural Heritage*. Green Bay, WI: Brown County Agricultural Bicentennial Committee, 1976.

Radisson, Pierre Esprit. *Early Native Peoples, Explorers, Traders, and Settlers: Arrival of the First Europeans, 1659–1660*. Edited by Gideon D. Scull. Boston: Prince Society, 1885. www.wisconsinhistory.org/topics/radisson.

Reaves, Shiela. *Wisconsin: Land of Change, an Illustrated History*. Sun Valley, CA: American Historical Press, 2004.

Schaefer, Joseph. *A History of Agriculture in Wisconsin*. Madison: State Historical Society of Wisconsin, 1922.

Schultz, L.H. *History of the Dairy Science Department, University of Wisconsin–Madison*. Madison: Board of Regents, University of Wisconsin System, 2009.

*Seventy-five Years of Farm Bureau in Wisconsin*. Madison: Wisconsin Farm Bureau Federation, 1994.

Smoot, Frank. *Farm Life: A Century of Change for Farm Families and Their Neighbors.* Eau Claire, WI: Chippewa Valley Museum Press, 2004.

Stone, Fanny, ed. "George Engelhardt" and "Edward Brice." *Racine: Belle City of the Lakes and Racine County, Wisconsin, a Record of Settlement, Organization, Progress and Achievement.* Vol. 2. Chicago: S.J. Clarke Publishing Company, 1916. http://www.archive.org/stream/racinebellecity02ston/racinebellecity02ston_djvu.txt.

Upper, Christen, comp. "Forest Pathology." Chap. 9 by Robert Patton, Forest Towns Advocated, in *With One Foot in the Furrow: A History of the First Seventy-five Years of the Department of Plant Pathology at the University of Wisconsin-Madison.* Edited by Paul H. Williams and Melissa Marosy. Dubuque, IA: Kendall-Hunt Publishing, 1986.

Williams, Paul H., and Melissa Marosy. *With One Foot in the Furrow: A History of the First Seventy-five Years of the Department of Plant Pathology at the University of Wisconsin-Madison.* Dubuque, IA: Kendall-Hunt Publishing, 1986.

## *Magazines/Newspapers*

*Among Ourselves: A House Organ for the Staff of the College of Agriculture* 1, no. 4. "Fund Established" (April 7, 1923). University of Wisconsin–Madison.

*Among Ourselves: A House Organ for the Staff of the College of Agriculture* 1, no. 1. "Swiss Cheesemakers Dairy School" (March 5, 1923). University of Wisconsin–Madison.

Andrews, Edmund. "Patents: Breeding High-Volume Dairy Cows." *New York Times,* August 24, 1991.

Bohn, Belle Cushman. "Hop Cultural in Early Sauk County." *Wisconsin Magazine of History* 18, no. 4 (June 1935): 389. Wisconsin Historical Society.

*Borden Eagle.* "John LeFeber." November 1934.

Burns, Jane. "Executive Q&A: Jung Co. CEO Plants Seeds for Huge Growth." *Wisconsin State Journal,* April 24, 2011.

*Creamery and Milk Plant Monthly* 1, no. 1. "Creamery-Milk Plant News" (September 1912): 41.

*Creamery and Milk Plant Monthly* 1, no. 1. "Notices" (September 1912).

*Green Bay Press Gazette.* "Brown County Fair Opens." September 1, 1909.

Hofacker, Cynthia. "Selling the Farm." *Eau Claire Leader Telegram,* December 31, 1999.

"John LeFeber, President of Wisconsin's Largest Milk Distributing Organization." No. 5 of a series on prominent men in the dairy industry, publisher/date unknown. Clipping courtesy of LeFeber's grandson, Bill LeFeber.

Johnson, Ron. "It's Time to Put Down Roots in Crawford County." *Dairy Star*, February 11, 2012, 31.

Knutsen, Kristian, and Ellen J. Meany. "Tobacco in Wisconsin: A Timeline, a Rich History in Agriculture, Business and Regulation." *Isthmus*, September 23, 2010.

Luther, H.L. "Farmers' Institutes in Wisconsin, 1885–1933." *Wisconsin Magazine of History* 30, no. 1 (September 1946): 59–68.

*Oshkosh Northwestern*. "Value of Farm Institutes." As reported in *Among Ourselves: A House Organ for the Staff of the College of Agriculture* 1, no. 2 (March 15, 1923). University of Wisconsin–Madison.

Pound, Glenn. "There's No Turning Back." *Madison Capitol Times*, December 11, 1978.

*The Rotarian* 5, no. 2. "Items of Interest" (August 1914): 92. International Association of Rotary Clubs.

Russell, H.L. *Among Ourselves: A House Organ for the Staff of the College of Agriculture* 3, no. 4 (October 29, 1924). University of Wisconsin.

Walters, Dorothy V. "Devil-Wagon Days." *Wisconsin Magazine of History* 30, no. 1 (September 1946): 69–77.

*Waukesha Daily Freeman*. "Farm for Sale." March 14, 1949.

*Wisconsin Agriculturist*. "Benefits of Green County." August 20, 1903, 3.

———. "Breeding Mares." April 19, 1900, 7.

———. "Buying a Farm." April 19, 1900, 15.

———. "Choice Farm Land for Sale." August 13, 1903, 11.

———. "Digging Potatoes." July 5, 1900, 5.

———. "Fertilizing Orchards." August 13, 1903, 9.

———. "Judging Sows." April 19, 1900, 7.

*Wisconsin Magazine of History* 18, no. 2. Documents and Gardner Letters (1934): 204–5.

*Wisconsin State Journal*. "Gov. Philipp Pays Tribute to Hoard." November 22, 1918.

———. "Wisconsin Ban on Margarine Targeted for Repeal." September 20, 2011.

# *Miscellaneous*

Adkinson, Thomas, Secretary. Rotary Club of Milwaukee meeting minutes, May 16, 1918. Rotary Club of Milwaukee archives.

Albenberg, Lester, Secretary. "Canned Food." Milwaukee Rotary Club meeting reminder, February 29, 1924.

Anderson, Christopher, and Diane Mayerfeld. "Cover Crops Case Studies: Gary Sommers Farm." Center for Integrated Agricultural Systems. Madison: Cooperative Extension Publishing, University of Wisconsin–Madison, January 2012.

Babcock, Stephen Moulton. "A New Method for the Estimation of Fat in Milk, Especially Adapted to Creameries and Cheese Factories." *Agricultural Experiment Station (AES) Bulletin* 24 (July 1890): 4.

Baker, Charles M., comp. "Gardner Letters." Wisconsin Historical Collections, vi, 463–64.

Baker, Hugh P. "The Woodpile: An Address to the Milwaukee Rotary Club," February 15, 1921. Meeting minutes, Rotary Club of Milwaukee archives.

Christensen, Chris. "What Place Has Culture in the Life of the Farmer?" Excerpt from an address at the Wisconsin Council of Agriculture Get-Together Conference, Madison, Wisconsin, November 1, 1939.

Coon, F.W. "The Ins and Outs of Tobacco Culture." Presentation to the State Agricultural Convention, February 1885, Madison, Wisconsin.

Faville, Stephen. "History of the Cheese Industry in Wisconsin." Wisconsin Cheesemakers' Association, ninth annual meeting, 1901.

Hatch, K.L. "Agriculture's Triple Seal." *Wisconsin Circular 193*. Agricultural Experiment Station Annual Report, February 1926.

Hatch, K.L., ed. "Organize for Dairy Marketing." *Wisconsin Circular 145*. Agricultural Extension Service. Madison: College of Agriculture, University of Wisconsin, May 8, 1914.

Henry, William. "Biennial Board Report, 1902–1903." University of Wisconsin Board of Regents, 67.

Hill, George W., and Ronald A. Smith. *Man in the "Cut-Over": A Study of Family-Owned Resources in Northern Wisconsin*. Agricultural Experiment Station Research Bulletin 139. Washington, D.C.: University of Wisconsin, Cooperating with Rural Surveys Section, Works Progress Administration, April 1941.

Hoard, William. "Meeting Minutes," Wisconsin Dairymen's Association Convention, 1872.

Houlihan, Tamas. "Full Spud Ahead: WPVGA Celebrates 60th Anniversary." Wisconsin Potato & Vegetable Growers Association, 2008.

Marschall Dairy Laboratory. "Cheesemaking in Wisconsin: A Short History," 1924. http://digital.library.wisc.edu/1711.dl/WI.Cheesemaking.

Moore, James G. "Some Recorded Facts Relative to the Development of Agriculture in the University of Wisconsin." Master's thesis, University of Wisconsin–Madison, 1955.

*Newsletter of the Civil War Round Table of Milwaukee.* General Orders No. 11-11 (November 2011): 6–7.

NFO news release. "National Farmers Organization Members Re-elect Olson as President." February 2, 2012.

Olson, Paul. "National Farmers Organization Supports Bargaining Rights." NFO news release, February 21, 2011. www.facebook.com/note.php?note_id=10150100954439484.

Pound, Glenn. "U.S. Agriculture and World Food Needs." Address presented to the Central Symposium of the University of Illinois, October 18, 1967. Found in *Pound Speeches* in UW Archives, Notebook 1, page 17.

Russell, H.L. "Report of the Dean of the College of Agriculture." *Board of Regents Biennial Report*, 1918.

Russell, Patrick. "Grandpa Russell's Own Story of His Life." Notes dictated to Mary Loretta Russell Lynch, July 10, 1916.

Silva, Erin, Laura Paine, Matt Barnidge, Cris Carusi and Ruth McNair. "Organic Agriculture in Wisconsin: 2012 Status Report." UW–Madison Center for Integrated Agricultural Systems and the Wisconsin Department of Agriculture, Trade and Consumer Protection, February 2012.

Smith, John Mills. "Why I Am a Horticulturist." Horticultural Society Report, 1887.

Stortroen, Anders Jensen. Letter from Martell Township, Wisconsin, autumn 1858.

The Tobacco Institute. "A Chapter in America's Industrial Growth: Wisconsin and Tobacco." Tobacco History Series, North Carolina State University Libraries, 1960.

United States Department of Agriculture. *Agriculture Yearbook*. Washington, D.C.: Government Printing Office, 1924.

Winnebago County, Wisconsin County Agricultural Agent. "Annual Report." Winnebago County, Wisconsin, 1944.

Wisconsin Farm Bureau membership brochure for Chris Christensen, former dean, College of Agriculture, University of Wisconsin–Madison, 1946.

Wisconsin State Board of Agriculture. "Annual Report of the Wisconsin State Board of Agriculture." Madison, Wisconsin, 1910.

Zondag, Richard. "Address to Employees, Customers, Business Associates and Friends." In *J.W. Jung Seed Company Centennial Commemorative.* Randolph, WI: J.W. Jung Seed Company, 2007.

## Websites/Web Documents

Alice in Dairyland. http://datcp.wi.gov/Business/Alice_in_Dairyland/Alice_Fast_Facts/index.aspx.

American Breweriana. "The Pabst Brewing Company." http://www.americanbreweriana.org/history/pabst2.htm.

Cheng, L., and P.D. Mitchell. "Status of the Wisconsin Ginseng Industry. Department of Agricultural and Applied Economics." University of Wisconsin–Madison, February 2009. http://www.aae.wisc.edu/pubs/misc/docs/Mitchell.WI.Ginseng.Industry.2009.pdf.

Clark County, Wisconsin Internet Library Project, photographs. http://wvls.lib.wi.us/ClarkCounty/pinevalley/tragedies/index.htm.

College of Agricultural & Life Sciences, University of Wisconsin–Madison. "CALS History." http://www.cals.wisc.edu/about-cals/history.

The Dan Patch Historical Society. "Dan Patch." http://www.danpatch.com.

Fromm Bros. Historical Preservation Society. "The Fromm Brothers' Story." http://www.frommhistory.org.

Ginseng Board of Wisconsin. "About the Ginseng Board." http://www.ginsengboard.com/aboutus.cfm.

Gorst Valley Hops. "History of Wisconsin Hops." www.gorstvalleyhops.com/history.php.

Honeywell, Alice. "La Follette and His Legacy." Wisconsin State Historical Society and the Robert M. La Follette School of Public Affairs, 1984. http://www.lafollette.wisc.edu/publications/otherpublications/LaFollette/LaFLegacy.html.

*Huffington Post.* "World's Largest Pumpkin 2010." October 22, 2010. http://www.huffingtonpost.com/2010/10/22/worlds-largest-pumpkin-20_n_772294.html.

Lemke Seed. http://www.lemkeseed.com.

Lincoln, Abraham. "Milwaukee Speech," September 30, 1859. United States Department of Agriculture, National Agricultural Library. http://riley.nal.usda.gov/nal_display/index.php?info_center=8&tax_level=4&tax_subject=3&topic_id=1030&level3_id=6723&level4_id=11085.

Lone Acres Farm & Moraine Airedales. "A Few of Our Cows." http://www.moraineairedales.com/aboutdairycows.htm.

Midwest Organic and Sustainable Education Service. "2008 Farmers of the Year—Gary, Nicholas & Rosie Zimmer." *The Organic Broadcaster*, March–April 2008. http://www.mosesorganic.org/attachments/news/foy08.html.

Racine History. "Racine History Timeline, 1699–1899," 2000. www.racinehistory.com/timeline.htm.

Reilly, Michael R. "McKerrow Family History." Sussex-Lisbon Area Historical Society, June 14, 2011. http://www.slahs.org/genealogy/families/mckerrow.htm.

Schwarze, Stan. "1933 Clark County Milk Strike." Clark County, Wisconsin, Internet Library. wvls.lib.wi.us/ClarkCounty/clark/history/1933MilkStrike.htm.

United States Department of Agriculture, National Agricultural Statistics Services. "2009 Wisconsin Dairy Goat Industry Overview." October 2009. *http://www.nass.usda.gov/Statistics_by_State/Wisconsin/Publications/Dairy/dairygoats.pdf.*

University of Wisconsin Extension. "History of UW Extension." http://www.uwex.edu/about/uw-extension-history.html#timeline.

Washington Island website. "Washington Island Business Directory," 1910, and information from L. Gordon's "Washington Island Insights" visitor guidebook, reprint, 1988. www.washingtonisland.com/visitors-guide/island-history-culture.

Wikipedia. "Henry Cullen Adams." http://en.wikipedia.org/wiki/Henry_Cullen_Adams.

———. "Henry Wallace." http://en.wikipedia.org/wiki/Henry_Cantwell_Wallace.

Wisconsin Cheese Information. "Join Us On a Tour of Wisconsin's Storied Cheesemaking Past." http://www.eatwisconsincheese.com/wisconsin/history_of_wisconsin_cheese.aspx.

Wisconsin Dairy Goat Association. "About WDGA." http://www.wdga.org/widairygoatassoc/about+wdga/default.asp.

Wisconsin Farm Bureau Federation. "Founding of the Wisconsin Farm Bureau." http://wfbf.com/about-wfbf/farm-bureau-faq.

Wisconsin Historical Society. "Henry Cullen Adams." http://www.wisconsinhistory.org/dictionary/index.asp?Submit=Search&action=search&keyword=Legislation.

———. "That's Meat and Drink to Me: Wisconsin's Malted Milk Story." www.wisconsinhistory.org/museum/exhibits/horlicks.

Wisconsin History. "The Babcock Test." http://www.wisconsinhistory.org/turningpoints/search.asp?id=705.

Wisconsin State Cow Chip Throw and Festival. http://www.wiscowchip.com.

Wisconsin State Cranberry Growers Association. "Cranberry Facts." http://www.wiscran.org.

# About the Author

Martin Hintz, author of *Forgotten Tales of Wisconsin* and *A Spirited History of Milwaukee Brews and Booze* with The History Press, has written about one hundred books for various publishers (Lerner, Capstone, Arcadia, Scholastic, Globe Pequot, Franklin Watts, Voyageur, Trails, Big Earth and others) on various topics. These include *Celebrate the Legend: 25 Years of Milwaukee Irish Fest* (Milwaukee Irish Fest, 2005); *Got Murder? The Shocking Story of Wisconsin's Notorious Killers* (Trails Publishing, 2007); *Wisconsin Cheese: A Cookbook and Guide to the Cheeses of Wisconsin* (Globe Pequot, 2008); and *Off the Beaten Path: Wisconsin* (Globe Pequot Press, 1989, with various reprints).

Articles published in major newspapers and consumer and trade periodicals include those in the *Chicago Tribune*, the *New York Post*, the *Chicago Sun Times*, *National Geographic World*, *Irish Music* magazine, *Where to Retire* magazine, *American Heritage*, *Interval*, *American Archaeology*, the *St. Petersburg Times*, the *Wisconsin Academy Review*, *Billboard*, *Amusement Business*, *Midwest Express* magazine, the

*Belfast News, City Lifestyle, Northshore Lifestyle, Dodge Van* magazine, *Jewish Heartland, Travel Holiday, Corporate Report Wisconsin, GolfWeek, Milwaukee* magazine, *Shepherd Express,* the *Daily Herald,* the *Jewish Chronicle,* the *Writer, Midwest Living, MotorHome, Meetings California, Dig, Michigan Living, Home & Away, M* magazine, *Group Travel Leader, Bus Tour* magazine and numerous others.

He and his wife, Pam Percy, operate Pampered Produce, a small farm in northern Milwaukee County. Members of the Wisconsin Farm Bureau, Milwaukee Urban Gardens and the Slow Food movement, they raise vegetables and chickens for eggs in a Community Shared Agriculture (CSA) program, serving more than twenty clients during the growing season. Pam has written two books on chickens: *The Complete Chicken* (Voyageur Press, 2005) and *A Field Guide to Chickens* (Voyageur Press, 2006). They collaborated on the Wisconsin cheese cookbook for Globe Pequot and also write regularly about food issues, chefs and restaurants for a number of magazines. For more than a decade, the couple has reported on Milwaukee's social/nightlife scene in a column, "Boris & Doris on the Town," for the *Shepherd Express* newspaper.

www.ingramcontent.com/pod-product-compliance
Lightning Source LLC
Chambersburg PA
CBHW060752100426
42813CB00004B/787